A Guide to Further Education
in England and Wales

CW00969909

Also available from Cassell:

P. Ainley: *Class and Skill*
L. B. Curzon: *Teaching in Further Education* (4th edition)
L. Glover: *GNVQ Into Practice*
P. Hodkinson and M. Issitt: *The Challenge of Competence*
T. Hyland: *Competence, Education and NVQs*
P. Lunneborg: *OU Women*
P. Mizen: *The State, Young People and Training*
A. Rogers: *Adults Learning for Development*
D. Thomas: *Flexible Learning Strategies in Higher and Further Education*

A Guide to Further Education in England and Wales

Leonard Cantor, Iolo Roberts and
Beryl Pratley

CASSELL

Cassell
Wellington House   215 Park Avenue South
125 Strand   New York
London WC2R 0BB   NY 10003

First published 1995

British Library Cataloguing-in-Publication Data
A catalogue record for this book is available from the British Library.

ISBN 0-304-33132-5 (hardback)
       0-304-33134-1 (paperback)

Typeset by Action Typesetting Limited, Gloucester
Printed and bound in Great Britain by Redwood Books, Trowbridge, Wiltshire

Contents

List of Abbreviations and Acronyms

ABC	*A Basis for Choice*
ACAC	Awdurdod Curiculum ac Asesu Cymru (National Curriculum Council for Wales)
ACER	Association of Colleges in the Eastern Region
ACM	Association of College Managers
AfC	Association for Colleges
AFE	Advanced further education
ALBSU	Adult Literacy and Basic Skills Unit
APC	Association of Principals of Colleges
APEL	Accreditation of prior and experiential learning
APL	Accreditation of prior learning
APVIC	Association of Principals of Sixth Form Colleges
ARELS	Association of Recognized English Language Schools
AS	Advanced Supplementary
ATL	Association of Teachers and Lecturers
BAC	British Accreditation Council for Independent Further and Higher Education
BEC	Business Education Council
BTEC	Business and Technology Education Council
BSI	British Standards Institute
CACC	Council for the Accreditation of Correspondence Colleges
CAT	Credit accumulation and transfer
C&G	City and Guilds
CBI	Confederation of British Industry
CCABC	Cyngor Cyllido Addysg Bellach (FEFCW)
CEDEFOP	European Centre for the Development of Vocational Training
CEE	Certificate of Extended Education
CEF	Colleges' Employers' Forum
CNAA	Council for National Academic Awards
CPVE	Certificate of Pre-Vocational Preparation
C3A	Colleges of the Third Age
DES	Department of Education and Science

DFE	Department for Education
DLF	Demand-led funding
DTI	Department of Trade and Industry
ED	Employment Department
EDUCA	The Digest for Vocational Education and Training
EEC	European Economic Community
EMFEC	East Midlands Further Education Council
EOC	Equal Opportunities Commission
ERA	Education Reform Act of 1988
ESOL	English for Speakers of Other Languages
EVB	Examining and validating bodies
ESRC	Economic and Social Science Research Council
FEDA	Further Education Development Agency
FEDOR	Federation of the Regions
FEFC	Further Education Funding Council for England
FEFCW	Further Education Funding Council for Wales
FEMIS	Further Education Management Information System
FERA	Further Education Research Association
FESC	Further Education Staff College
FEU	Further Education Unit
FFORWM	Welsh Colleges Forum
GCE	General Certificate of Education
GCSE	General Certificate of Secondary Education
GNVQ	General National Vocational Qualification
HEFC	Higher Education Funding Council
HEFCW	Higher Education Funding Council for Wales
HMI	Her Majesty's Inspectors
IIP	Investors in People
IIP UK	Investors in People United Kingdom Ltd
LASER	London and South Eastern Regional Advisory Council
LEA	Local education authority
LEC	Local Enterprise Council (Scotland)
LSE	London School of Economics
MIS	Management information system
MSC	Manpower Services Commission
NACETT	National Advisory Council for Education and Training Targets
NAFE	Non-advanced further education
NAO	National Audit Office
NASD	National Association for Staff Development
NATFHE	National Association of Teachers in Further and Higher Education
NCC	National Curriculum Council

NCVQ	National Council for Vocational Qualifications
NEBAHAI	National Examinations Board for Agriculture, Horticulture and Allied Industries
NEWI	North East Wales Institute of Higher Education
NFER	National Foundation for Educational Research
NOCN	National Open College Network
NROVA	National Record of Vocational Achievement
NVQ	National Vocational Qualifications
OCNs	Open College Networks
OSC	Occupational Standards Council
OFSTED	Office for Standards in Education
OHMCI	Office of Her Majesty's Chief Inspector
PDAG	Pwyllgor Datblygu Addysg Gymraeg (Welsh Language Education Development Committee)
PEI	Pitmans Examinations Institute
PGCE	Post-Graduate Certificate in Education
PIC	Private Industry Council
PICKUP	Professional, Commercial and Industrial Updating
RAC	Regional advisory council
RSA	Royal Society of Arts
SCAA	Schools Curriculum and Assessment Authority
SCOTVEC	Scottish Vocational Education Council
SEAC	Schools Examination and Assessment Council
Skill	The National Bureau for Students with Disabilities
SRHE	Society for Research into Higher Education
TA	Training Agency
TDLB	Training and Development Lead Body
TECs	Training and Enterprise Councils
TEED	Training, Education and Enterprise Directorate
TRADEC	Trades Education Courses
TUC	Trades Union Congress
TVEI	Technical and Vocational Education Initiative
UDACE	Unit for the Development of Adult and Continuing Education
UPDC	Universities' Professional Development Consortium
UVP	Unified Vocational Preparation
UCET	University Council for the Education of Teachers
WJEC	Welsh Joint Education Committee
WLB	Welsh Language Board
WRFE	Work-related further education
YTS	Youth Training Scheme

Preface

This book follows in the line of the series of books on further education in England and Wales which the first two named authors have written during the past twenty-five years. We were emboldened to write this book partly because, most fortunately, we were joined by Beryl Pratley, an experienced and authoritative practitioner and writer on the further education scene. However, while this book follows our previous books on the subject, it is completely new, in itself a measure of the enormous changes which further education has undergone since we last put pen to paper almost ten years ago. We also embarked on this formidable project in the expectation that since the major legislation of the 1992 Further and Higher Education Act came into effect, the sector would be granted a degree of stability. Now, a year or so after we began, that looks much less certain with further changes looming in the shape of staff redundancies and possible college mergers, to mention but two. To that extent, therefore, this book is a snapshot of the further education sector in England and Wales as we see it at the beginning of 1995. We hope, nevertheless, that it will provide an account of the context in which the sector operates as well as a detailed description of the varied important functions which further education performs.

We trust this book will be of interest to students who are studying education, irrespective of the field of educational practice they may later choose to enter; to teachers, both in further education and in the school and higher education sectors; to business people and industrialists who have special interests in this field; to the makers of education and training policy, including politicians and administrators, and to interested lay persons.

Finally, although the conclusions we draw and any errors and omissions we have made are our own, we wish to express our appreciation to the following, who have allowed us to make use of their knowledge and who have, in a variety of ways, helped us to write this book: Roy Ainscough, Chief Executive, East Midlands Further Education Council; Eric Ashton; Jim Bennet, FEU Officer for Wales; Dr Frank Foden; John Griffiths and Arfon Rhys, Coleg Menai, North Wales; Dr William Hall, Executive Director, National Centre for Vocational Education Research, Australia; Dr M. Jones, Secretary to the Board of FFORWM; Merfyn Morgan, Education and Training Division of the Welsh Language Board; Sheila Pickard and Graham Pickering, Further Education Funding Council for Wales; Alwyn Rowlands, Gwent College of Higher Education; Don Scott, Honorary Secretary, National Association for Staff Development in Post-16 Education; Brenda Shaw, Education Department, Loughborough University; Janet Smith of the Council of TECs in Wales; Adam Suddaby, Vice Principal, Charles Keene College, Leicester; and Andrew Young, Chief Executive, Association of Colleges in the Eastern Region.

Loughborough, Keele and Kingston,   *Leonard Cantor*
January 1995   *Iolo Roberts*
                                                        Beryl Pratley

One

Further Education in the 1990s

In writing about the further education sector in England and Wales, we have in previous books been describing a sector whose definition had remained unchanged for decades: namely all forms of post-school education, except that provided by the universities.[1] The sector, so defined, was normally subdivided into advanced further education (AFE) and non-advanced further education (NAFE), the former consisting of all courses leading to a final qualification above the General Certificate of Education (GCE) Advanced Level or its vocational equivalent, such as Business and Technology Education Council (BTEC) National Certificate and Diplomas, and the latter consisting of all courses leading to a final qualification up to and including GCE A-level or its vocational equivalent. The sector covered a field of great diversity embracing a wide variety of institutions, the great majority of which were under local education authority (LEA) control. The main providers of AFE, or public sector higher education as it was called, were the polytechnics and colleges and institutes of higher education, while the main institutions providing primarily non-advanced courses were the colleges of further education, or technical colleges, and tertiary colleges, which offered, as they still do today, a broad range of programmes, including those which are vocational in purpose, those which cater for general education, and those which comprise a wide range of leisure and cultural activities. In addition, there were, and are, a smaller number of specialist institutions like colleges of art and design and colleges of agriculture and horticulture offering courses covering a restricted range of subjects. Finally, a major part of the further education sector was made up of thousands of adult education centres of one form or another offering a wide range of recreational courses.

It is a measure of the changes that have taken place in further education in so short a period as the last five years or so, resulting directly from government legislation, that the relatively long-standing definition of further education described above no longer obtains. This legislation, including especially the 1988 Education Reform Act and the 1992 Further and Higher Education Act, is examined later in this chapter. Meanwhile, as a result of its passing, further education in England and Wales now consists

1

of three major types of institutions: further education colleges, including specialist institutions such as colleges of art and design and colleges of agriculture and horticulture; tertiary colleges; and sixth-form colleges (Figure 1.1). Together, they comprise a new sector of education, numbering some 500 colleges and educating over 2,800,000 students. In other words, since 1 April 1989, when the provisions of the 1988 Education Reform Act took effect, the polytechnics, as they then were, and the colleges and institutes of higher education moved out of the further education sector and out of LEA control. In this way, the so-called 'seamless robe' of further education, whereby the whole range of courses from those for young people leaving school at 16 with no academic qualifications through to those leading to post-graduate qualifications was available in the same sector and whereby, in theory at least, students could progress through them, was irreparably broken. Since then, of course, the polytechnics and a few of the institutues of higher education have been granted university status.

The three major types of institution presently comprising further education – further education colleges, general or specialist; tertiary colleges; and sixth-form colleges – have somewhat different characteristics, though they also have much in common, especially in regard to the first two, and these common features are likely to become more marked in the years ahead. General further education colleges, which number 229 in England and about 20 in Wales, offer, as we have seen, a broad range of courses and cater for students of all ages from 16 onwards. They provide annually for some 1,700,000 students, 60 per cent of whom are over the age of 19, the majority attending on a part-time basis. Until 1 April 1993, when the provisions of the 1992 Further and Higher Education Act came into effect, they were maintained by their respective LEAs; on that date they became state-supported corporations financed largely through two funding councils, one for England and one for Wales, which are directly responsible to the Secretaries of State for Education and Wales respectively. As we shall see later, the two funding councils have adopted somewhat different working arrangements. The consequences of this 'independence' for the management of the colleges and the new roles of the governors and senior management teams are considered in detail later in the book. However, one interesting development that has followed their independent status is that, partly because of the merger of some colleges but mainly to improve their image and signal the break with the local authority, an increasing number of colleges have changed their names and adopted new logos. Usually this has meant dropping the words 'Technical' or 'of Further Education' from their titles. Occasionally, however, they have adopted a completely new title, as in the case of Warrington Collegiate Institute, formerly the North Cheshire College of Further Education.[2]

Specialist further education colleges number about 50 in England

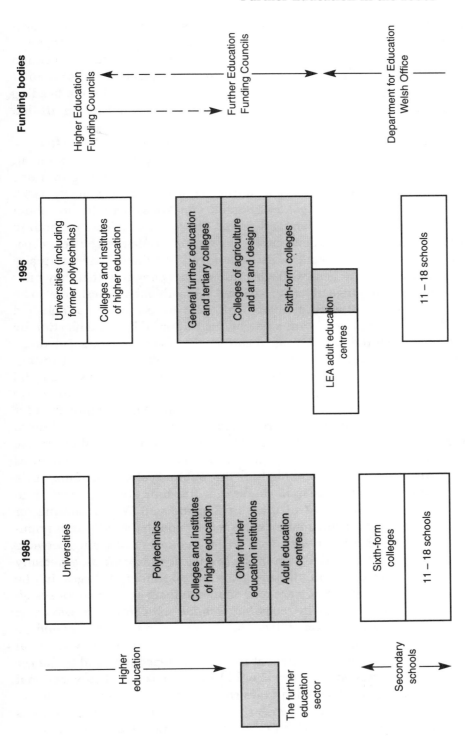

Figure 1.1: *The Changing Structure of Further Education in England and Wales, 1985 to 1995*

Wales; some 36 concentrate on providing courses in agriculture and horticulture, and 14 specialize in art, design and the performing arts. Together they account for about 10 per cent of the students in the further education sector.[3] However, a number of general further education colleges offer courses in aspects of agriculture and horticulture, often under the heading of land-based studies, and most of them make some provision in art and design.

Tertiary colleges, the first of which were established in the 1970s, are institutions which, in theory and very largely in practice, cater for all students aged 16 and above in a given area, thereby combining into one college both school sixth-form and further education provision. By 1992, there were 67 tertiary colleges in England and Wales, catering for about 450,000 students, most of them part-time.[4] They vary considerably, both in size and character. Some concentrate largely on academic courses, especially GCE, while others, the majority of them, are virtually indistinguishable from general further education colleges in that they offer in addition a wide range of vocational and recreational courses. Like some further education colleges, a number of them have recently established 'franchising' arrangements with a nearby institution of higher education by which they teach the early stages of certain first degree courses. However, what perhaps distinguishes them most from the traditional general further education college is that the average age of their students is lower and the fact that they attach particular importance to the needs of the 16 to 19 age group. In recent decades, many LEAs sought to make separate provision for this age group and one popular response was the creation of sixth-form colleges, largely in order to concentrate resources which would otherwise have been split between separate sixth forms. Run under school regulations until 1 April 1993, they combined all the public sector sixth forms in a given area and offered academic courses for full-time students aged 16 to 19. In 1994, there were 117 of them in England and Wales, catering for some 116,000 students or about a quarter of the country's sixth-form population. They are smaller in size than tertiary colleges, averaging between 600 and 700 students, and the emphasis is on academic courses, especially GCE A-level. Indeed, with the inclusion of sixth-form colleges in the further education sector there are now more students aged 16 to 19 studying for GCE A-levels than in secondary school sixth forms. However, in recent years many sixth-form colleges have broadened their intakes and, to cater for less academically inclined students, have introduced vocational and pre-vocational courses. Now that they are 'independent' and no longer subject to school regulations, they should be able to extend their vocational provision and, should they wish to do so, their adult education provision. However, expansion may well be restricted by lack of finance and facilities and, indeed, many may not wish to alter their traditional character. Finally, if we accept the definition of the further education sector as those institutions receiving funds from the funding councils, then there are two major categories which should be mentioned. The first comprises institutions described by the funding councils as 'Designated Institutions'; these include certain adult education colleges and specialist institutions such as the National Sea Training College and Cordwainers College. In 1992–93, between them they enrolled some 175,000 students. The second comprises students undertaking further education courses in higher education institutions, very largely the former polytechnics: there were some 14,000 of them in 1992–93.

Although, in analysing the nature of the further education sector in England and Wales, we have restricted ourselves almost entirely to those institutions previously maintained by the LEAs and now largely funded by the funding councils, there is also a significant *private* or *independent sector of further education*, of which brief mention must be made. The most recent, if necessarily somewhat imprecise, information available is to be derived from a survey of independent further and higher education in Great Britain conducted in May 1992.[5] At this time, there were some 3000 independent 'college-type institutions' who registered nearly 600,000 students, of whom 296,000 were studying full-time. Of the total of nearly 600,000, 58 per cent were female and more than 95 per cent were taking further education courses. The independent sector of further education was predominatly located in England, which had 2745 colleges, while Wales had 110. The most popular subject areas were business studies, which accounted for 18 per cent of the students, computing with 9 per cent, and engineering and technology and medical related, each with 8 per cent. Also with significant numbers were construction, English as a foreign language, for overseas students very largely, and the creative arts. By comparison with the publicly funded further and higher education sectors of Great Britain, the independent sector accounted for about 13 per cent of the total student population.

As there are no specific standards which the private colleges have to meet, or any requirement to register themselves with the Department for Education (DFE) or any other body, the reputation of the colleges and the quality of the programmes which they offer necessarily vary a great deal. Moreover, as they are directly subject to market forces, some of them come and go in response to supply and demand. There are, however, some organizations concerned with the standards of the independent sector of further education. These include the British Accreditation Council for Independent Further and Higher Education (BAC), the Council for the Accreditation of Correspondence Colleges (CACC) and the British Council through the Association of Recognized English Language School (ARELS), which accredits English language schools. As participation in these accreditation schemes is entirely voluntary, only a small proportion of independent colleges belong to them. Nevertheless, given the very substantial numbers of students attending them, their contribution to the national provision of further education is clearly important.

Government policy towards the publicly funded further education institutions, as codified in recent legislation, has, as we have seen, wrought enormous changes. The first major piece of legislation we shall deal with is the Education Reform Act of 1988 (ERA). Although most public attention was focused on its implications for primary and secondary education, nevertheless those for further and adult education were far-reaching.[6] One of the main thrusts of this and subsequent legislation was to strip LEAs of their powers to control their colleges, a policy which culminated in the provisions of the 1992 Further and Higher Education Act. In the meantime, the ERA required LEAs to delegate financial responsibility to the governing bodies of institutions with an enrolment of 200 or more full-time equivalent students, which in practice encompassed virtually all the further education and tertiary colleges in England and Wales. At this stage, the sixth-form colleges remained part of the school sector, though a similar delegation of financial responsibility was also required there. The governing bodies of the further education colleges were reconstituted, becoming smaller than before, with at least one half of their members independent both of the local authority and of the college, a high proportion from industry, no more than 20 per cent representing the local authority, and no more than two members of the college staff. In this, as in certain other respects, the government seems to place considerable faith in the ability of members of industry to oversee effectively the provision of further education and training. Within a year of the passing of the Act, a Report by Her Majesty's Inspectors (HMI)[7] stated that local authorities had already implemented new arrangements for college governance in accordance with its provisions and that between three-quarters and four-fifths of total further education funding had been delegated to the colleges. In the following year, a survey of 177 further education colleges by the Further Education Staff College (FESC) revealed that the newly constituted boards of governors were indeed smaller than before, their members were predominantly white and 47 per cent of them were from industry and business.

Like virtually all post-war governments before them, the Conservative administration of recent years has rightly felt the need to grapple with Britain's relatively poor record on skills training. Their broad objective has been to develop a system of vocational education and training which will produce a workforce that is sufficiently flexible and adaptable to respond positively to economic and technological changes, thereby enabling Britain to compete more effectively in world markets.[8] In order to achieve this aim, the government has felt it necessary to intervene directly in vocational education and training policy and, inevitably perhaps, has emphasized training rather than education. Consequently, the Employment Department (ED) and, to a lesser extent, the Department of Trade and Industry (DTI) have become closely involved in making policy, taking initiatives and setting training standards.

Back in 1981, the government published its White Paper, *A New Training Initiative: A Programme for Action*,[9] which set out a programme for improving training, including the setting of a target date of 1985 for achieving recognized standards for all the main craft, technician and professional skills to replace time-serving and age-restricted apprenticeships. At the core of this initiative was an attempt to make explicit the desirable outcomes to be obtained from vocational education and training.[10] Achieving these objectives was, of course, another matter and the next major stage in the uphill journey was the publication in 1986 of the White Paper, *Working Together: Education and Training*,[11] issued jointly by the Department of Education and Science (DES) and the ED, which reinforced the government's aim of establishing standards of competence. To promote this objective, the White Paper recommended the establishment of the National Council for Vocational Qualifications (NCVQ), which duly occurred in the same year. It was given the remit of producing a rational progressive structure of vocational qualifications and of increasing substantially the proportion of the workforce who held them. A target date of 1991 was set by which this framework should be in existence. From the outset, NCVQ adopted the principle that vocational qualifications were to be obtained by the demonstration of 'competencies', that is standards of performance, so that what were important were outcomes. When approving awards submitted to it by the examining and validating bodies for the award of National Vocational Qualifications (NVQs), this would be the major criterion. Inevitably, this stance evoked strong resistance from many in the further education sector and in the examining and validating bodies who felt that it would result in curricula that left out essential learning which develops understanding. As we describe in detail in Chapter 3, although a degree of compromise has been reached, the argument over this fundamental issue continues.

Then in December 1988, the government issued yet another White Paper, *Employment for the 1990s*, whose main strategy was clearly put:

> Above all we must invest in skills and knowledge of our people and build up industry's skill base through a strategy of training through life, to enable Britain to continue to grow and generate jobs. The prime responsibility for this investment lies with employers.[12]

Accordingly, following the proposals in the White Paper, a nation-wide network of 82 Training and Enterprise Councils (TECs) in England and Wales and 20 Local Enterprise Councils (LECs) in Scotland has been established. They are local bodies funded by the ED to foster economic growth by promoting and sponsoring training. After varying degrees of consultation with the education service, primarily the further education and tertiary colleges, they have drawn up strategic plans for the provision of training in their local areas, mainly youth training and employment training for jobless adults formerly provided under programmes funded nationally by the Training Agency (TA) and its successor, the Training, Enterprise and Education Directorate (TEED) of the ED. In addition, until 1994 when the funds were channelled through the funding councils, the TECs were given financial control of the 25 per cent of work-related further education in the colleges which was formerly funded by the TA. Clearly, the TECs are intended to play a major role in the planning, designing and delivery of vocational education and training. The establishment of fruitful working relationships between them and the further education sector is therefore very important and the working out of these relationships is examined in detail later in the book.

In the following year, 1989, both the Trades Union Congress (TUC), through its publication, *Skills 2000*,[13] and the Confederation of British Industry (CBI), through the report of its Vocational Education and Training Task Force, expressed the view that it was imperative to modernize the British system of vocational education and training and to establish clear and explicit standards within vocational qualifications. The CBI report, *Towards a Skills Revolution – A Youth Charter*,[14] proposed a set of 'common learning outcomes', or core skills – namely communication, problem-solving, personal skills, numeracy, information technology and modern language competence – which should be achieved by all 16- to 19-year-olds. This concept of core skills was endorsed by the DES when it asked the National Curriculum Council (NCC) and the School Examination and Assessment Council (SEAC) to consider how they could be incorporated into GCE Advanced and Supplementary Levels, culminating into the publication by the NCC of its 1990 report, *Core Skills 16–19*,[15] in which it recommended that they be incorporated in the study programmes of all 16–19-year-olds. At about the same time, the NCVQ issued a report, *Common Learning Outcomes: Core Skills in A/AS Levels and NVQs*,[16] in which it endorsed the NCC recommendations. Thus, the intention is that the inculcation of these core skills will provide a sound base for both academic and vocational education and training.

The next major pronouncement on the further education sector appeared in May 1991 with the publication of the White Paper, *Education and Training for the 21st Century*,[17] released jointly by the DES, the ED and the Welsh Office. Among other things, its proposals were designed to end what it described as 'the artificial divide' between academic and vocational qualifications, to stimulate more young people to train through the offer of a training credit, to promote the role of employers in education through the TECs and, last but not least, to give the colleges more freedom to expand their provision and respond more flexibly to the demands of their customers. To achieve these aims, it proposed that all further education and tertiary colleges be given independence from their LEAs and that the same should apply to sixth-form colleges, which would be transferred to the new further education sector. It is interesting to note that the White Paper holds up tertiary colleges as institutions which were offering the full range of academic and vocational courses for all young people in their areas and which were proving to be very successful in attracting students.[18] Instead of being largely funded by the LEAs, as from 1 April 1993, the colleges would receive their public funds through two new funding councils appointed by and responsible to the Secretaries of State for Education and Wales respectively. They would be termed further education funding councils (FEFCs), one for England and one for Wales, and would be assisted in their decisions by a network of regional advisory committees. As far as the governance of the colleges themselves was concerned, they would be established as corporate bodies with powers to employ their own staff and manage their own assets and resources. The college governing bodies given these powers would contain a representative of the local TEC but not of the LEA, seemingly a somewhat spiteful provision. The TECs would be given extra responsibilities, including working with the funding councils and the colleges, so that their involvement in the management of further education would be strengthened.

As far as qualifications were concerned, new broad-based courses known as General National Vocational Qualifications (GNVQs) would be introduced by September 1992. The intention was to recognize the wish of many young people to keep their career options open by studying for vocational qualifications which prepare them for a range of related occupations but do not limit their choices too early and enable them if they wish to move into higher education.[19] This new qualification was designed to supplement the job-specific National Vocational Qualifications (NVQs) being introduced by the NCVQ, which was in the process of 'hallmarking' qualifications submitted to it for approval by the awarding bodies which proliferate in further education. Thus, there would be three routes to high-quality qualifications available to young people: GCE A-levels; general vocational qualifications, comprising both existing BTEC awards and new GNVQs; and occupationally specific NVQs, approved by the NCVQ. Finally, where adult education was concerned, the new funding councils would support only a limited number of courses, including those leading to higher education, the acquisition of basic literacy, and proficiency in English for speakers of other languages and proficiency in Welsh. Significantly, and controversially, 'other provision', including leisure courses for adults, should as far as possible be supported through student fees and not by the funding councils. These far-reaching and very important proposals were duly incorporated more or less in their entirety in the 1992 Further and Higher Education Act and have now come into effect. Much of the rest of this book is concerned with how they are working out in practice.[20]

The introduction of the NCVQ framework, mentioned above, and the gradual accreditation of vocationally specific courses for the award of NVQs which has been taking place in the past five years or so, has also had repercussions for another important area of further education, namely that of teacher training. The NCVQ has adopted the attitude that teachers in further education and elsewhere who are teaching courses which lead to the award of NVQs should themselves have undertaken a training course which is 'competence-based'. Accordingly, the major providers of further education teacher-training courses outside the universities, namely the City and Guilds (C&G) and the Royal Society of Arts (RSA), have introduced new courses which are competence-based, and the universities themselves have been modifying their courses in this direction. These and other major developments in the field are examined in detail in Chapter 6.

Finally, in May 1994, the government published yet another White Paper, *Competitiveness: Helping Business to Win*,[21] whose recommendations, if they are implemented, will have far-reaching implications for the way in which further education colleges are financed. In 1990, a system of training credits was announced whereby those leaving full-time education at 16 or 17 should receive 'credits' with which to pay for their own training by purchasing it from a training organization of their choice. As we describe in Chapter 2, the scheme has met with only moderate success. However, the White Paper proposes that it be extended to all 16- to 18-year-olds who have left further education, though not without prior consultation before a decision is made on whether to embark on pilot schemes in 1995–96. If the proposal is implemented in its entirety it will bring about a radical change in the way that public money is spent on education and training and could further transform the manner in which colleges are funded. Another government proposal, restated in the White Paper, concerns national targets for education and training, first endorsed by the government in 1991. These include the objective, for example, of ensuring that four out of five young people reach Level 2 of NVQs by 1997, and that 50 per cent reach Level 3, the equivalent of GCE A-level, by the year 2000 (these targets were modified in May 1995).

Last, but not least, the government has stated that it is committed to transforming what it has described as the 'Cinderella' image of further education. It plans to increase the number of students in the sector by 25 per cent between 1993 and 1996, and in his autumn statement of 1992 the Chancellor of the Exchequer stated that the money would be made available to make this possible. Of course, it remains to be seen whether students will come forward in sufficient numbers and whether they will be adequately funded. There have been some encouraging signs: for example, figures issued in May 1993 indicated that more than 70 per cent of 16-year-olds were remaining in full-time education after the minimum school-leaving age, and a substantial proportion were in the further education sector. On the other hand, figures released by the Further Education Funding Council for England (FEFC) in February 1994 showed that most colleges were predicting that student numbers would expand only by just over 5 per cent in the current year compared with the target of 6.9 per cent. Much of the shortfall may be because many students enrol on courses whose fees are not paid by the FEFC and therefore do not count towards the targets the colleges have been set. Another contributory factor in some areas is that higher education institutions seem to have been poaching students from further education colleges, some of whom have lost 20 per cent of their students on higher education courses.[22] The question of adequate funding for would-be students may turn out to be even more problematical. In the spring of 1993, for example, principals of further education colleges were representing to the funding councils that the national target for increasing student numbers by 25 per cent over the next three years was being hampered because hard-pressed local authorities were making cuts in discretionary grants to students.[23] Particularly badly affected were agricultural colleges, whose students, as they cannot live at home, often rely on discretionary grants to cover their residential and travel costs. In addition, many other students are affected or likely to be so, including those on courses ranging from GCE A-levels to professional dance and drama. Indeed, it is estimated that in 1990, for example, more than 150,000 students received discretionary grants totalling more than 80 million. It is not surprising, therefore, that the cuts that are taking place are regarded by many in the educational service as a considerable threat to widening educational opportunities. This and other major issues concerning students in further education are examined in detail in Chapter 4. These and similar problems notwithstanding, it is at least heartening that at long last the government seems to have come to realize that the further education sector has a key role to play in the provision of education and training.

Notes and References

1   See, for example, L. M. Cantor and I. F. Roberts, *Further Education Today: A Critical Review*, London, Routledge & Kegan Paul, 1986 (3rd edn), p. 1.

2   'What's In a Name Change', *Furthering Education*, 1, 20–21 (1993).

3   Further Education Funding Council, *Quality and Standards in Further Education in England*, Chief Inspector's Annual Report, Coventry, 1993–94, FEFC, p. 19.

4   E. Macfarlane, *Education 16–19 in Transition*, London, Routledge, 1993, p. 15.
5   'Participation in Independent Sector Further and Higher Education in Great Britain', *Statistical Bulletin*, **25/93**, Department for Education, 1993.
6   See S. Maclure, *Education Reformed: A Guide to the Education Reform Act*, London, Hodder & Stoughton, 1989 (2nd edn); and M. Flude and M. Hammer, *The Education Reform Act, 1988: Its Origins and Implications*, London, Falmer Press, 1990.
7   Department of Education and Science, *The Impact of the Education Reform Act on Further Education: A Report by HMI*, London, DES, May 1990.
8   P. Raggatt and L. Unwin (eds), *Change and Intervention: Vocational Education and Training*, London, Falmer Press, 1991, p. xi.
9   Employment Department, White Paper, *A New Training Initiative: A Programme for Action*, Cmnd 8455, London, HMSO, 1981.
10 G. Jessup, *Outcomes: NVQs and the Emerging Models of Education and Training*, London, Falmer Press, 1991, pp. 10–11.
11 Employment Department/Department of Education and Science, White Paper, *Working Together: Education and Training*, Cmnd 9823, London, HMSO, 1986.
12 Employment Department, White Paper, *Employment for the 1990s*, Cmnd 540, London, HMSO, 1989.
13 Trades Union Congress, *Skills 2000*, London, TUC, 1989.
14 Confederation of British Industry, *Towards a Skills Revolution – A Youth Charter*, London, CBI, 1989.
15 National Curriculum Council, *Core Skills*, 16–19, London, NCC, 1990.
16 National Council for Vocational Qualifications, *Common Learning Outcomes: Core Skills in A/AS Levels and NVQs*, London, NCVQ, 1990.
17 For a full description of these developments, see ref. 8.
18 B. Tomlins and J. Miles, *Reorganizing Post-16 Education: The Tertiary Option*, NFER, Slough, 1991, pp. 87–88.
19 Further Education Unit, *Vocational Education and Training in Europe*, London, FEU, 1992, p. 30.
20 For a detailed account of the political background to the legislation which was enacted between 1988 and 1992, see W. Richardson, 'The 16–19 education and training debate: "deciding factors" in the British public policy process', Chapter 1, pp. 1–37, in W. Richardson, J. Woolhouse and D. Finegold (eds), *The Reform of Post-16 Education and Training in England and Wales*, London, Longman, 1993.
21 Employment Department/Department of Trade and Industry, *Competitiveness: Helping Business to Win*, Cmnd 2563, London, HMSO, May 1994.
22 D. Evans, 'Poached beyond palatability', *Times Educational Supplement*, 2 December 1994, p. 5.
23 J. Meikle, 'Axe falling on key services', *The Guardian*, 30 March 1993, p. 7.

Two

The Administration and Funding of Further Education

It is a measure of the enormous sea change which has taken place in the administration and funding of the educational system of England and Wales that less than a decade ago we could describe it as a 'national system locally administered', in other words it was essentially a partnership between the then Department of Education and Science, since retitled the Department for Education (DFE), the major partner and central authority, and the local education authorities (LEAs).[1] At that time the legal basis for this partnership was still supplied by the 1944 Education Act, together with various amending acts, which placed upon LEAs the responsibility for the allocation of grants to and the day-to-day running of the education service, including the further education sector. Since then, as we have seen in Chapter 1, a flood of legislation, especially the Education Reform Act of 1988 and the Further and Higher Education Act of 1992, has completely transformed the situation.

This transformation is largely the product of two basic tenets of faith of the Conservative governments which have been in office since 1979: their commitment to a market ideology, namely that educational standards were too low and could best be raised by greater enterprise and competition on the part of the colleges; and that many of the LEAs were politically and ideologically misguided and a bureaucratic hindrance to the raising of these standards. Hence, the 1988 Education Reform Act and subsequent legislation has effectively emasculated the LEAs and strengthened the central authority and, to an extent, individual colleges.[2]

Under the present system, the central authority's control over broad educational policy is, if anything, stronger than ever. This is well exemplified by the announcement in the autumn of 1992 that student numbers in the further education sector should grow by 25 per cent over the next three years and the consequent 'requirement' by the DFE that the colleges increase their populations by approximately 8 per cent in each of the three years from 1993 onwards. However, at the time of writing, it seems highly unlikely that sufficient numbers of students will come forward to enable these targets to be reached. Another example of a diktat from the DFE to the colleges is that their grants from the funding councils be cut by 3.5 per cent per year, the deficit being made up by 'efficiency gains'. From which precise sources such policy decisions emanate is not, however, entirely clear. While the DFE and the Welsh Office have overall responsibility for the educational system in England and Wales respectively, other agencies have a hand in determining policy towards education and training, notably the Prime Minister's Downing Street Policy Unit and the Employment Department (ED). As a consequence of recent legislation, the colleges no longer derive their funds largely from the LEAs, who in turn met the cost of running their colleges from the central government's Rate Support Grant and the local rates. Since the creation of the two funding councils, following the provisions of the 1992 Further and Higher Education Act, and the granting of 'independence' to the colleges on 1 April 1993, the funding councils have taken over from the LEAs the function of allocating public grants to the colleges. While these provide the major share of the colleges' finances, the latter also obtain funds from other sources, including other government departments, especially from the Training, Education and Enterprise Directorate (TEED) of the ED and directly from industry and business.

Thus, the national context in which the further education colleges operate has changed out of all recognition in recent years, and responsibility for policy-making and for funding them is shared by several bodies, including government departments, the funding councils and the Training and Enterprise Councils (TECs). The colleges' work is also, of course, influenced and determined to various degrees by other bodies, including the former regional advisory councils (RACs), the validating and examining bodies, the Further Education Unit (FEU) and the Further Education Staff College (FESC), and the further education teachers' and lecturers' organizations (Figure 2.1). Bearing in mind that the administrative structure and financial framework in which the colleges operate is a complex matrix, we shall endeavour to describe the main agencies operating in further education, nationally, regionally and locally.

The Department For Education (DFE)

Compared to other government departments, the DFE is relatively small and, as we have seen, is very largely concerned with educational policy. At the beginning of 1992, it moved out of its former premises at Elizabeth House on the South Bank into Sanctuary Buildings in Great Smith Street, which brings it nearer to Whitehall, which may or may not be seen as an advantage. It is headed by a secretary of state, who is a member of the cabinet, supported by a minister of state with responsibility for further and higher education, and a hierarchy of permanent civil servants. This contrasts with the position in Wales (see Chapter 7), where the responsibil-

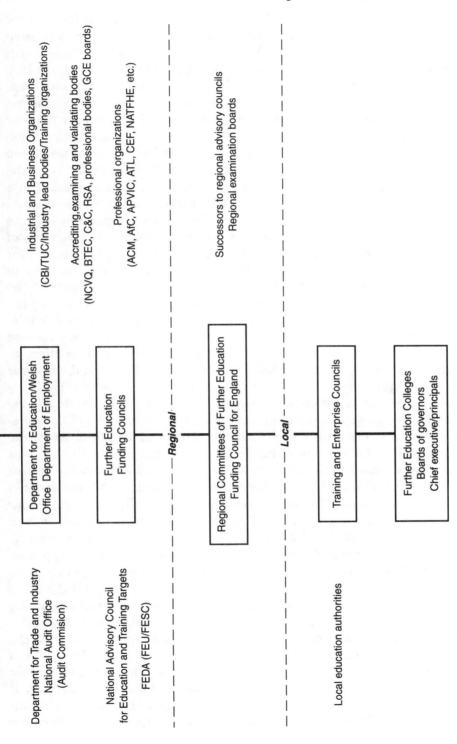

Figure 2.1: *The Administrative Framework of Further Education*

National

Department for Education/Welsh Office   Department of Employment

Further Education Funding Councils

Department for Trade and Industry
National Audit Office
(Audit Commision)

National Advisory Council
for Education and Training Targets

FEDA (FEU/FESC)

Industrial and Business Organizations
(CBI/TUC/Industry lead bodies/Training organizations)

Accrediting, examining and validating bodies
(NCVQ, BTEC, C&C, RSA, professional bodies, GCE boards)

Professional organizations
(ACM, AfC, APVIC, ATL, CEF, NATFHE, etc.)

Regional

Regional Committees of Further Education
Funding Council for England

Successors to regional advisory councils
Regional examination boards

Local

Training and Enterprise Councils

Further Education Colleges
Boards of governors
Chief executive/principals

Local education authorities

ity for education, as with Welsh affairs, generally rests with the Secretary of State for Wales, who is in charge of the Welsh Office, where he is assisted by two parliamentary under-secretaries, one of whom has specific responsibility for education. For further and higher education in England, the DFE has three separate policy branches: one concerned with higher education, one with further education, and one with student affairs, though it seems likely that the days of the last are numbered. Indeed, in September 1993 the secretary of state announced a review of the work and future organization of the DFE, to take into account the other organizational changes which have taken place, such as the establishment of the funding councils. At the time of writing, no announcement on the future structure of the DFE has been made,[3] so that at present the principal functions of the further education branch, which has shrunk considerably in size, are described by the DFE as comprising general policy on further education, the funding of further education through the Further Education Funding Council for England (FEFC), and policy on post-16 curriculum and qualifications in schools and further education in England. Among the specific matters to be considered under policy and funding are those relating to the FEFC and the promotion of the national education and training targets. Clearly, the relationship between the DFE and the FEFC is a crucial one, not least because the guidance issued by the secretary of state to the latter and its effect on the annual level of funding and how finances are distributed to the colleges is of great importance to the further education sector as a whole. This relationship is being worked out at present and will continue to develop, being influenced by, among other things, the personalities and views of the secretary of state and the chairman and chief executive of the FEFC. As for the national targets for education and training, which apply to the UK as a whole, these were put forward originally by the Confederation of British Industry (CBI), endorsed by the Trades' Union Council (TUC) and adopted by the government in 1991. There are eight targets in all, consisting of four 'foundation' targets aimed at young people aged between 16 and 18, and four 'lifetime' targets aimed principally at college and workplace training. The former include ensuring that, by 1997, 80 per cent of our young people will reach Level 2 of the National Vocational Qualification (NVQ) or its equivalent and that, by the year 2000, 50 per cent will reach NVQ 3 or its equivalent, such as GCE A-level, and the latter aim to provide training activities for all employees and to have half of all workers at NVQ Level 3 by the year 2000. These targets, which are closely directed towards NVQs, are due to be delivered by the TECs, together with the CBI, the TUC and business. However, as there is evidence that schools in particular are not very aware of them and as they have attracted little press coverage, it remains to be seen whether they will be achieved. Indeed, a report published early in 1994 by the National Advisory Council for Education and Training Targets, which was established in March 1993 with a membership spanning industry, the education service and government as an independent body to monitor and report publicly on progress towards the national targets, indicates that some of the most important of these targets are being missed and that much more effort is required from employers, schools and colleges if all the goals are to be reached by the year 2000.[4] Subsequently, in a discussion document issued in July 1994, it stated that if the UK is to compete with countries such as Japan and France then more ambitious targets should be aimed for. Meanwhile, the present targets are important insofar as they provide the framework for policy decisions by the DFE and also the ED and DTI which will influence the way in which government funding is channelled. Further emphasis is given to the importance which the government attaches to these targets in the White Paper, *Competitiveness: Helping Business to Win*,[5] issued in May 1994.

The student affairs branch of the DFE includes among its terms of reference considerations of 'existing arrangements and future policy on mandatory and discretionary awards in England and Wales'.[6] As we have seen in Chapter 1, the question of discretionary awards is an important one for further education, particularly given that, as a recent survey shows,[7] many students are refused financial support for courses which can be considered crucial to the economy. Nevertheless, there seems to be little likelihood that the government will change its attitude towards discretionary grants and fund them more generously.

However, there is one area in which the DFE has greatly increased its expenditure in recent years and that is on publications of various sorts, whether in glossy White Papers, which are white no longer, but multi-coloured, or on booklets such as *The Charter for Further Education* or *It's Your Choice: A Guide to Choosing at 16*.[8] These last two are useful publications: the charter explains to students what they have a right to expect from the colleges and other bodies, and announces that by 1994 every college will have developed its own charter; and the latter spells out the wide range of choice of qualifications available to 16-year-olds.

Until fairly recently, the DFE was served by Her Majesty's Inspectors (HMI), who acted as a field force in the oversight of all aspects of education, including further education, with Wales having its own inspectorate. HMI had a very important role in advising the DFE about the standards and effectiveness of further education provision and also carried out a programme of inspecting colleges so that all concerned – the central authority, the local authorities, and the colleges themselves – were kept informed of the quality and relevance of the work being undertaken.[9] However, during recent years the nature of the work of HMI gradually changed as they were used by the central authority primarily to report more broadly on developments in further education and the success or otherwise of government initiatives. Finally, in 1993 the inspectorate was rather brutally disbanded and alternative inspectorial arrangements were made. In the case of further education, the responsibility was handed over to the funding councils, who have made alternative arrangements, details of which are examined later in this chapter.

Responsibility for the education service in Wales, including further education, lies with the Welsh Office, and a detailed examination of its role is to be found in Chapter 7. Meanwhile, other government departments, notably the ED, and official bodies also influence the further education sector to different degrees.

The Employment Department (ED)

The role which the ED plays in the provision and funding of the further education sector is considerable and growing. Perhaps the most obvious source of influence is through the public money which it provides. This it does mainly by financing the TECs for their various programmes. However, as we shall see, it has also taken a variety of initiatives, sometimes in collaboration with the DFE and sometimes on its own, which strongly affect the colleges. On a day-to-day basis, its education and training activities are located at its Training, Enterprise and Education Directorate (TEED), which is situated in Sheffield. Set up in 1990, TEED was designed, among other things, to ensure that broad lines of government policy were imposed on the TECs and that their expenditure was limited. However, because of the policital sensitivity involved and the importance to the government that the TECs succeed, the control exerted by TEED seems to have been somewhat limited and, indeed, it has been described as 'collapsing into' the ED.[10]

That apart, the ED has in recent years taken a number of initiatives to stimulate skills training. In 1986, the then Training Agency (TA), the predecessor of TEED, established a major programme to foster more explicit standards of competence in employment. This included, as we have seen, establishing the National Council for Vocational Qualifications (NCVQ), and also a large number of so-called *lead bodies.* These lead bodies have as their prime function the identification and maintenance of occupational standards and the development of NVQs based on them. Initially, they were mainly industrial training organizations or bodies of employers representing individual industries.[11] Later, however, a number of occupations or industries came together to form lead bodies representing similar or overlapping areas, such as the Care Sector Consortium and the National Textile Training Group. More significant still, given that training and development are or should be common to the whole of the industrial and business sector, cross-sectional lead bodies have been established, of which the most important one for further education is the Training and Development Lead Body, known popularly as the TDLB. In the autumn of 1994, it was announced that the TDLB would soon become part of a new organizational structure, when it would merge with at least one related body to form a 'super' lead body to be known as the Occupational Standards Council, or OSC. The OSC will have overall responsibility for NVQs relating to personnel management and training and development. Meanwhile, the TDLB has been particularly important in working out the criteria and national standards for the so-called 'role competencies' of trainers and instructors leading to the award of NVQs. These were examined by the FEU and others to see if they were relevant to further education colleges, and it was concluded that they could be used for this purpose. By the early 1990s, over 150 lead bodies had been established and were engaged in developing standards for more than 500 different occupations. However, a significant omission from the plethora of lead bodies is the one for education, which should have been established along with the others and which, rather than the TDLB, should have produced the criteria upon which to base the award of NVQs to further education lecturers, trainers and instructors. However, the initial criteria for its establishment met with a good deal of criticism from the education service on the grounds that it placed too great an emphasis on training and took too narrow a view of education. Consequently, its setting up was deferred and a cynic might infer that there is no great enthusiasm from the ED for this to happen as the whole issue is politically very sensitive and, in the absence of any alternative, the criteria laid down by the TDLB were being adopted. However, it has been suggested that a further education lead body be established, thereby limiting its scope to a sector where education and training are clearly intertwined. Thus, in July 1993, the DFE wrote to interested parties a letter entitled 'National Vocational Qualifications: Lead Bodies and Education Service', arguing that as the further education colleges would be playing a major role in delivering NVQs and were well placed to explain to employers the value of such competence-based qualifications, 'it would be helpful if the FE sector could be seen to be supporting the implementation of such qualifications for their own staff'. In other words, if the further education sector were 'attracted to the construction of a system of relevant qualifications' for its staff, then the setting up of an appropriate lead body might be a first step. The letter also concludes that it was not necessary to consider lead bodies for other groups of staff in the education service, e.g. in the schools and higher education. This somewhat restricted view of the role of an education lead body, while it might not take a broad enough view of the needs of education and training, is a compromise which may well prove acceptable to the DFE and ED. However, it leaves something to be desired, not least by creating or reinforcing artificial boundaries between further education and the other sectors of the education system, and by bringing about a duplication of standards in qualifications 'which differ in context rather than in function or process'.[12] The latest development is that at the end of 1994 the DFE and ED instructed the new Further Education Development Agency (FEDA), which supersedes the FEU and the FESC in April 1995, to take the first steps towards the establishment of a further education lead body which, among other things, will be given the task of setting out criteria for new competency-based teaching qualifications for staff in further education colleges.

Another potentially important initiative first supported by the CBI and later taken up by the ED is the introduction of training credits, or youth credits. First announced in March 1990, the credits are designed to enable youngsters leaving full-time education at 16 or 17 to pay for part-time vocational education and training by buying it from an approved training organization of their own choice. The principal aims of the scheme, which was launched as a major solution to the country's youth training problems, are to enable young people to make their own choice of career, to give them more opportunity to choose their training programmes, and to give them a sense of the cost of their training.[13] Started on an experimental basis with a limited number of TECs in 1992, by its second year it was displaying a number of teething troubles, according to a report published by the National Foundation for Educational Research (NFER). Among them were administrative complexities, problems with TEC funding to further education colleges and a disappointing take-up by young people. One complaint of the colleges was that the private sector providers were weaning off the better trainees, leaving the colleges with a higher proportion of trainees with lower ability who needed considerable help and support for which they were inadequately financed by the TECs. It also seems to be the case that some employers are reluctant to give young people time off for training so that they are unable to 'cash' their training credits. The original intention was that by 1996–97, every 16- or 17-year-old leaving full-time education will be entitled to receive a training credit. However, at the end of 1993, in conjunction with a proposed new apprenticeship scheme, it was announced that they would be made available a year ahead, in 1995–96. Even if this comes about, it seems unlikely that the offer will be taken up by large numbers of young people and experience so far suggests that the training credits have done little to widen their choice of training or increase their ability to search out the best opportunities. However, the principle of giving young people an entitlement to enhance their careers has been generally welcomed and many employers seem to look upon the scheme with favour, seeing it as giving some financial benefits to their companies.

The success or otherwise of the youth credits programme will necessarily depend in part on providing young people with high-quality careers guidance and this is another area over which the ED has been given control. At present, the only providers with the legal responsibility to do so are the LEAs. Believing that local authority control has resulted in a framework that is rigid, unresponsive to change and lacking impartiality, the government through the 1993 Trade Union Reform and Employment Rights Act brought the careers service under the control of the ED. Certainly, some local authorities have funded their careers services more generously than others, and partly as a consequence some are better than others. Equally, the stated aim of the government, to raise the standards of all the services to those of the best, is laudable enough. Whether the new arrangements will bring about such a highly desirable result is, of course, another matter. The principle upon which the new arrangements is based is that the creation of a free market in careers guidance will lead to higher standards. Accordingly, in 13 pilot or 'pathfinder' areas in England, would-be providers, including the private sector, were invited to submit bids by December 1993 so that successful bidders could be notified to commence provision in April 1994. Interestingly enough, this is in contrast to both Wales and Scotland, where the secretaries of state explicitly invited the local authorities, in partnership with their local TECs, to bid for the work on the understanding that private providers would be approached only in the event of the LEA–TEC partnership being unable or unwilling to submit bids, an unlikely contingency. Meanwhile, in England it seems that not a single bid has come forward from the private sector and consequently all the contracts have gone to the local authorities, either on their own or in partnership with their local TECs. During the next two years, bids will be invited for the remaining areas of England and it may well be that the private sector may decide or be induced to put forward proposals.[14]

Inevitably, the changes that are taking place have created insecurity among the established local authority careers service, and some of the detailed arrangements, which, for example, link payment to the number of young people seen, are felt to be detrimental to the interest of individuals. Moreover, the financial restrictions which have been imposed on local authority funding make many feel that the official aim of raising all services to the level of the best is unlikely to be realized. Whatever the present difficulties and uncertainties, it is to be hoped that an effective and efficient careers service will emerge, for without it the promise of sound careers guidance for all young people who need and want it will not be realized and their future careers will be put at risk.

Another initiative put forward by the ED at the end of 1993, which if it proves successful will clearly have an impact on the further education colleges, is the so-called 'modern apprenticeship' scheme. It will be run using the current youth credits scheme, which will become nationally available to all 16- and 17-year-old school leavers in September 1995, a year sooner than originally planned. Traditional apprenticeships, once one of the main routes into skilled training, involved young people in learning a trade for a fixed period, often for five years, and were prominent in such areas as construction and the manufacture of metal goods. However, apprenticeships have been declining in number for many years, partly because of industry's needs to reduce costs and to introduce flexibility and partly through technological change. Although the details have yet to be fully worked out, the new-style apprenticeships will, according to the government, no longer be based on time-serving, but on the idea of a joint commitment, or pledge, by the apprentice and his or her employer to a significant period of training leading to high standards of competence, normally a NVQ 3, the vocational equivalent of GCE A-level, and will extend to new sectors of industry not previously covered by them. The scheme, which will be designed by individual industry training organizations in collaboration with TECs, started on a pilot basis in September 1994 when 2000 school leavers began apprenticeships in 14 industrial sectors, including agriculture, business administration, engineering construction, information technology and travel services. It is hoped to add many more sectors a year later, when the scheme should become fully operational with about 40,000 new places annually. The scheme will be funded over a period of three years, at a cost of £1.25 billion, by which time between 120,000 and 150,000 'modern apprentices' are expected to be receiving training. In addition, the government announced in its May 1994 White Paper, *Competitiveness – Helping Business to Win*,[15] that the programme would be extended to cover 18- to 19-year-olds, from April 1995, on an accelerated modern apprenticeship scheme which aims to produce by the end of the decade 30,000 technicians and crafts people training to Level 3 of NVQ each year. Meanwhile, the existing scheme attracted a mixed response, with some trainers contending that it is little more than an attempt by the ED to promote the use of training resources which are inadequate and under-resourced. Put forward by the government as one of the most important components in its drive for a better trained, highly skilled workforce, it remains to be seen whether it will achieve the dimensions hoped for.

Also, as part of its strategy for improving the quality of training for the workforce, the ED has promoted the activities of Investors in People (IIP), which provides industrial and other organizations with a standard or 'kitemark' by which to judge the quality of the people who work for them. IIP has subsequently become Investors in People UK Ltd (IIP UK) and has set up a special working party to foster its use in schools and colleges. It claims that by the spring of 1994, 70 per cent of further education establishments had committed themselves to achieve its standard and that 50 of them had already reached it.[16]

Finally, the ED finances a major research programme, most of which is commissioned, to promote the development of its initiatives in vocational education and training. Some idea of the scope of this programme can be gained from its *Annual Report on Research*, which in 1994, for example, listed its research projects under a variety of headings, including youth and education, operations, training strategy and infrastructure and adult learning. Among the interesting projects are an evaluation of the second year of the pilot schemes for training credits, undertaken by the NFER, resulting in the publication in 1993 of its *Evaluation of the Second Year of Training Credits*,[17] an evaluation of work-related further education by the Policy Studies Institute; and a baseline study of six TECs by Coopers and Lybrand to assess their performance, influence and impact.

It is clear from this description of its various activities which impinge upon the further education sector that the ED is playing a larger and larger role in determining and financing vocational training. It has been suggested a number of times in the past decade or two that in order to develop a properly coordinated national programme of education and training it would be desirable to merge the DFE and those parts of the ED concerned with training, and there is no doubt, as will be seen from the foregoing account, that there has been an increasing trend towards common and sometimes competing interests. Whether such a merger would result in the promotion of a more streamlined policy or whether it might over-emphasize training at the expense of education is very much open to question.

Finally, two other government departments which have some influence on the work of the colleges, albeit less directly than the DFE and the ED, are the Department of Trade and Industry (DTI) and the Department of the Environment. The DTI has necessarily a stake in government policy on skilled training and has played its part in helping to determine it, not infrequently resulting in departmental rivalry. In the past decade, the Department of the Environment through the Audit Commission, which was responsible for judging the efficiency of bodies funded by local government, has from time to time examined the way in which resources have been utilized in the colleges. In 1985, for example, its publication *Obtaining Better Value from Further Education*[18] concluded that better use of colleges' resources could be brought about by more efficient management and made a number of detailed recommendations, some of which aroused the ire of many in the colleges. Then in 1987 it was highly critical of the then Manpower Services Commission's (MSC) adult training strategy, which was designed among other things to give training to and to find work for the long-term unemployed, arguing that it was slower and more expensive than provision in the further education colleges.[19] Finally, in 1993 it published *Unfinished Business: Full-time Educational Courses for 16–19 year olds*,[20] a study undertaken jointly with HMI. Designed primarily to advance the development of quantitative techniques for measuring performance and costs in colleges and schools, it concluded that current levels of non-completion of courses by students were unacceptably high in many institutions and made a number of recommendations for improving the situation. Recently, the National Audit Office (NAO), which assesses the use of nationally administered funds, has taken over the Audit Commission's functions with respect to further education, since the local authorities no longer fund the colleges and the FEFC, which provides them with the bulk of their finances, is a national organization outside local authority control. Indeed, the 1992 Further and Higher Education Act gave the NAO powers to inspect colleges' accounts and to carry out value for money studies in the sector. Consequently, in the course of 1994 the NAO began to institute a number of visits to further education colleges as part of its responsibility to ensure that they deliver value for public money. Following each visit, the college concerned will receive a report which will not be published. However, general conclusions reached as a result of the visits will be summarized in an annual report to be submitted to the House of Commons Public Accounts Committee, and the first report was due to be published in February 1995. Although the NAO has stated that these visits should be looked upon by the colleges as a matter of routine, it seems inevitable that they will increase the bureaucratic burden upon them and cause a degree of trepidation. The NAO is also currently examining the systems of controlling their finances employed by the TECs, following reports that they had submitted incorrect claims for funds to the ED. It is also about to undertake a value for money study of the FEFC, followed by its Welsh equivalent and colleges in the Principality.

The Further Education Funding Councils

As we have seen, the 1992 Further and Higher Education Act included among its provisions the setting up of two funding councils, one for England and one for Wales, which would take over 'full responsibilities for funding institutions in the new further education sector on 1 April 1993'. We shall deal first in detail with the Further Education Funding Council for England (FEFC) and then consider the differences between it and the one for Wales (FEFCW).

In July 1992, the then education secretary, John Patten, announced the membership of the FEFC and also wrote to its chairman, giving broad guidance on its functions and setting out particular matters to which he expected the FEFC to have regard. The FEFC is chaired by Robert Gunn, former chairman of the Boots Company plc, and has 13 other members, all nominated by the education secretary. The FEFC's chief executive, Sir William Stubbs, was formerly chief executive of the now defunct Polytechnics and Colleges Funding Council. The members are drawn largely from industry and business and from further education. The main duty of the FEFC is to provide a 'coherent funding regime for further education in England' and in doing so to 'strike a balance between securing maximum access to the widest possible range of opportunities in further education and avoiding a disproportionate charge on public funds'. It should also, as Section 9 of the Act requires, make provision for assessing the quality of education in its further education colleges and to this end establish a quality assessment committee. It should work closely with the TECs, ensure that college finances and financial management are soundly based and that the needs of the students with learning difficulties are met, and, last but not least, it should make certain that new funding arrangements should not impose an undue administrative burden on the colleges, a requirement that many would contend is more honoured in the breach than the observance. The FEFC would be assisted in these Herculean tasks by the establishment of regional committees whose role is to advise it on 'local issues related to its duties and powers and on local factors which affect funding requirements'.

Immediately upon its establishment, the FEFC set to work to create a financial framework within which the colleges would operate, covering audit arrangements, accounting procedures and financial forecasts. In this context, Sir William Stubbs has explicitly stated that it is not the FEFC's intention to control what the colleges do or how they are managed, or to interfere in the curriculum, though all these areas are bound to be affected by the financial criteria that are established. Certainly, the FEFC was very quickly into its stride and in the 18 months from its establishment until the end of 1993 issued some 70 circulars, an average of one a week, most of them requiring quick responses from the colleges. As a senior member of a college commented, this proliferation of paper, if it continues, will take up many college hours just in handling FEFC correspondence.[21] A substantial document sent out by the FEFC to the colleges at the end of 1992 was *Funding Learning*,[22] outlining six different ways in which it might allocate its funds and inviting comments on its proposals. While the document is reasonably clear and readable, many of the FEFC circulars have generated a language and jargon relatively new to the colleges. Terms like demand-led funding (DLF), high core funding, lower marginal funding rates, and rates of convergence, and, of course, their financial implications for college management, have led college governors, managers and teaching staffs to spend much time informing themselves and seeking elucidation of these rather arcane subjects.

Having set in hand a lengthy consultation process, following the publication of *Funding Learning* and subsequent circulars, about the funding methodology to be adopted, the FEFC had by the end of 1993 arrived at a provisional new funding system to be introduced if possible in September

1994. The system is a complex one which broadly divides student learning into three sections — described as 'entry', 'on-programme', and 'exit' or 'achievements' — comprising the volume of each college's provision which could be expressed in 'standard units' upon which funding would be based. The system also includes units for additional support to the colleges and, where appropriate, the remission of fees to students. The FEFC has established a tariff advisory committee which will monitor and review the volume of each college's provision and propose any new changes. In this way, it can effect changes in provision by increasing or decreasing weighting for different subject areas or types of courses. The FEFC also wants the colleges to adopt what it calls a 'mode-free' approach to funding, whereby instead of as at present having no fewer than seven categories of attendance — ranging from full-time, through sandwich to part-time day release and evening only — there will be only two categories for all courses, full-time and part-time. Some idea of the complexity involved can be gathered from the fact that the adoption of such a classification would require the listing on a national basis of part-time programmes and their associated unit values.[23] This gives only a brief outline of a complicated methodology which the FEFC proposes to base its funding. It is scarcely surprising that it has required a great deal of assimilation and understanding by colleges, who did, however, vote in favour of this particular formula out of a number put forward by the FEFC. It will also require the colleges to supply the FEFC with a great deal of detailed information, and the extent to which the new system becomes fully operational will depend on the availability of additional funding for the installation of management information systems and the relevant software. On the other hand, the present system of funding leaves something to be desired and its replacement by a fairer one would be welcomed by the colleges.[24] Whether that will come about, and when, remains to be seen.

As we have seen, the funding councils have been given other responsibilities in addition to providing a coherent funding regime for further education in England and Wales, prime among them being to assess the quality of education in further education and, to that end, to set up a quality assessment committee. This was done quickly, and in order to link its funding decisions with judgements about quality, the FEFC decided to establish its own inspectorate. A chief inspector, Terry Melia, a former Chief HMI, has been appointed, as have a number of both full-time and part-time inspectors, drawn from a variety of backgrounds, including HMI, further education colleges, TECs, industry and business. The intention was to have 70 full-time inspectors in post and 600 part-timers trained and registered by July 1995, who will be based and work in the FEFC's nine regions. In April 1993, the FEFC issued a consultation document, *Assessing Achievement*, which outlined the proposed framework for the inspection of colleges, and invited reactions from the further education sector, reactions which on the whole were favourable.[25] The system of inspection will operate at three levels: each college will be assigned its own inspector; teams of inspectors with specialist knowledge and experience will examine specific curriculum areas and such things as special needs provision; and the college will be formally inspected across its whole range of activities once every four years. The first two forms of inspection will result in unpublished reports to the college for its own use, and the third will produce a published document. The new system of inspection will differ from the former, carried out by HMI, in two important respects: firstly, as part-time inspectors can be drawn from college staff, it will include an element of peer review, like that of the former Council for National Academic Awards (CNAA), in which colleges and their staff are judged, in part at least, by their peers in other colleges; and secondly, the inspectors will report to the FEFC quality assessment committee and not to the Secretary of State for Education – though how much difference will result in practice remains to be seen. In preparation for these visits, colleges will need up-to-date prospectuses, college charters, development plans, and strategic plans, as indicated in *Assessing Achievement.* The visits will result in reports which, among other things, will grade the curriculum areas of the college and aspects of its cross-college provision, such as its governance and management, from 1 to 5. Grade 1 will denote an area which has 'many strengths and few weaknesses' and Grade 5 'many weaknesses and very few strengths'. However, no grade will be assigned to the college as a whole.

Clearly, the system will involve a great deal of bureaucracy, if perhaps less than was previously the case, and, in some cases, call for the judgement of Solomon. However, its importance should not be underestimated. The FEFC has made it clear that it will use the results of 'sector-wide inspection' to 'inform funding decisions' as well as highlighting and encouraging good practice, and identifying strengths and weaknesses.[26] Meanwhile, the round of inspections has begun in earnest and up to 120 reports should have been issued by autumn 1995 as a result of the visits. In addition to reporting on individual colleges, the FEFC inspectorate also issues an annual report in which it comments on the general state of the further education sector. Its first report was published towards the end of 1994 and was based on inspections of no fewer than 11,000 lessons involving 150,000 students. While acknowledging that the sector was 'dynamic, responsive and entrepreneurial' and that teaching was, on the whole, sound and well founded, it nevertheless urged the colleges to improve unacceptably high drop-out rates on some courses, to cut some of the teachers' administrative duties and to provide more extracurricular activities for students. It also highlighted the desperate need to provide better accommodation in the shape of teaching rooms and new common rooms and refectories.

The Further Education Funding Council for Wales (FEFCW) operates in broad terms in a similar fashion to its English equivalent. However, there are at least two significant differences. Firstly, its chief executive is also chief executive of the Higher Education Funding Council for Wales, although it and the FEFCW are separate bodies. Secondly, it funds many fewer institutions and organizations, 37 in all, made up of further education, tertiary and sixth-form colleges and a group of other institutions and bodies, including the four Welsh Colleges and Institutes of Higher Education for their students attending further education courses, Coleg Harlech, the adult education college, the North and South Wales branches of the Workers' Educational Association and the Young Men's Christian Associations in Wales. In addition, for a maximum period of 16 months from 1 April 1993, it funds the Welsh Colleges Forum (FFORWM) and three regional 'access consortia', which provide 'access' courses in colleges for mature students wishing to enter higher education. As is the case in England, some higher education institutions in Wales currently provide further education, previously funded by the LEAs, and responsibility for funding this provision has been taken over by the FEFCW. The FEFCW's terms of reference are similar to those of its English counterpart – for example, it too has set up a quality assessment committee – but, in addition, it is required to take into account the need for Welsh language provison. It has also established close working relationships with other important bodies in Wales and has reciprocal observer status with the FEFC. It issued its own consultative document, *Funding FE in Wales*,[27] in September 1993 which, like its English equivalent, recommended a rapid move towards funding units of learning. A more detailed examination of its progress to date is to be found in Chapter 7.

The Regional Advisory Councils (RACs)

Further education has differed from other sectors of our education system in having a regional dimension in the form of regional advisory councils (RACs). Until recently, there have been ten of them, nine in England and one, the Welsh Joint Education Committee (WJEC), for Wales. In the last few years, however, like virtually every other aspect of further education, they have undergone a major transformation, resulting in them ceasing to be advisory bodies and in the disappearance of one of them, the West Midlands RAC. In their previous incarnation, RACs had a number of functions, the chief of which was to advise their constituent local authorities and the further education colleges in their regions on the needs which had to be met in relation to all aspects of further education and to seek to coordinate provision in the regions. They also provided a forum for the exchange of ideas among the further education institutions and between them and industry, business and government agencies and higher education; made known the facilities available in the region by publishing directives, bulletins and reports; organized short courses, conferences and seminars; and encouraged the training and staff development of further education teachers. In addition, they provided and conducted examinations and assessments and awarded certificates at craft and operative level. As we shall see, under their new guise, they still perform some of these functions. They were originally established by cooperation between the local authorities in their regions and were financed by them. They were therefore dominated by their LEAs, who were in effect their owners. However, within the last few years the local authorities have ceased to fund them and one after another the former RACs have become independent companies with charitable status, inheriting from their constituent local authorities both their assets and liabilities.

As independent companies, they have to ensure that they remain solvent and have striven to replace LEA funding from other sources. In typical instances such as EMFEC (East Midlands Further Education Council) and LASER (London and South Eastern Regional Advisory Council) – acronyms and initials now seem *de rigeur* – their funds derive from membership fees; from subventions of various kinds; from the conduct of examinations, though these are declining; from training events, such as programmes for the training of verifiers for City and Guilds (C&G) further education teachers courses (see Chapter 6) and for teachers in schools offering General National Vocational Qualification (GNVQ) programmes; from project and consultancy work, such as Euro-Unit, which produces up-to-date information about the various funding programmes relevant to vocational education and training, links with partners in other European countries, and help and advice in adding a European dimension to the vocational education and training curriculum;[28] from extensive programmes of conferences and seminars; and from the sale of their publications, including compendia and directories of further education provision in their areas. They still provide regional forums for discussion of matters of importance to further education and training, as contributing members include representatives from further education colleges, higher education institutions, LEAs, industry and business. They also typically provide an information service in one form or another; in the case of EMFEC, for example, this comprises specialized databases and a library of teaching and learning materials relevant to the needs of colleges and other individuals and organizations operating in the vocational education and training sector. Finally, the eight RACs have launched a new Federation of the Regions, known as FEDOR, which since it was established in September 1993 has taken two significant initiatives. The first is the compilation of a national picture of events designed to support training and adult development organized by the eight companies in 1993, and the second is the introduction of a new quarterly publication devoted specifically to the needs and interests of the vocational education and training sector, entitled *Furthering Education*. Judging by its first issue, which appeared in the autumn of 1993, it promises to be both informative and interesting.

And what of their future? Undoubtedly, the RACs were disappointed that when recent legislation reshaped the further education sector they were not included in the new formal arrangements. However, by and large they have been successful in recasting themselves into independent charitable companies and in continuing some of their former functions, as well as taking up new ones. In the absence of any regional structure for further education – except for the regional committees of the funding councils, which in theory at least have no planning function – there is no one left to provide a regional strategy and colleges are being left at the mercy of market forces to sink or swim by themselves. However, because of this situation they need help and support, especially consultancy services, and the new transmogrified RACs, albeit in competition with many others, are in a good position to offer them. Perhaps, before too long, the colleges, and perhaps even the government, will come to realize that there is a need for a regional advisory and planning structure. It is, therefore, not without significance that feeling in need of a regional forum in which to exchange views and represent them at regional and national levels, a group of college principals, or chief executives as they now call themselves, in the eastern region of England have come together to form ACER (Association of Colleges in the Eastern Region) which, like FFORWM in Wales, is a partnership of further education corporations 'established in order to enable colleges to respond successfully to the challenges of incorporation and beyond'. At the time of writing, its membership comprises 23 out of the 41 further education colleges in the former RAC region but no sixth-form or agricultural colleges. Among its activities are staff development work with senior college staff and a recent joint conference with funding council inspectors. It will be interesting to see if ACER's example is followed by colleges in other regions.

The Local Education Authorities (LEAs)

As we have seen, the role of the LEAs in providing and financing further education has, since the provisions of the 1992 Further and Higher Education Act came into effect, greatly diminished. Now that the colleges receive the bulk of their public funds from the funding councils, such moneys as they obtain from the LEAs are restricted to a few categories.

These comprise: some traditional adult education, including what is termed 'non-Schedule 2' work, that is provision other than the largely vocational work which is closely specified in Schedule 2 of the Act; some discretionary awards to students to attend courses in the colleges; and subsidies for enabling students to travel to and from college. As far as discretionary awards are concerned, the situation is increasingly unsatisfactory as, due to financial stringency, more and more LEAs are cutting back on them or in some cases making none at all. As a result, across the country significant numbers of students are dropping out of courses, for example mature students on access courses, because they can no longer afford to continue. Concern in the colleges about the situation has led the DFE and the FEFC together with two charities, to fund the NFER to undertake a survey of the subject. The report, which was published in April 1994, stated that overall spending on discretionary grants was thought to have fallen by 8 per cent in 1993 and that there were striking differences between the policies adopted by individual local authorities. These findings may well lead to a full-scale inquiry into the future of the awards and their administration. In the meantime, the payments to students to travel to and from college are also becoming more restrictive, so that in some cases they are only financed to travel to their local college, thereby limiting their choice.

In order to oversee and assist their further education colleges, the LEAs have until recently had an administrative structure which provided services of different kinds, including, for example, the maintenance of the colleges and their grounds. In addition, some authorities appointed professional advisers specifically to help their colleges on curricular and other matters. Since the colleges have become independent they can buy in help from the LEAs for maintenance or other services, or not as they choose, and many, perhaps most, colleges have turned elsewhere to private providers, leaving local authority provision much reduced. Moreover, the professional officer structure of the LEAs has now disappeared, the officers concerned having either retired or obtained other posts in the colleges, the schools or with bodies such as the funding councils. As a consequence, the periodic authority-wide meetings of college principals which were organized by many LEAs have also gone, though some college principals do arrange meetings on an informal basis.

A residual problem which has lingered on in some local authority areas is that at the time of incorporation a number of colleges were in debt to their LEAs, occasionally for very considerable sums, and these debts have still not been paid off. The dispute is particularly acute in Coventry, where two further education colleges are in debt for very considerable amounts of money and where the city councillors are threatening to take legal action to force the FEFC to clear them. This places the FEFC in a considerable dilemma: on the one hand, it can scarcely stand by and see colleges go under, particularly in areas like Coventry, where the training they provide is vitally important to the city's economy; yet, on the other, it does not wish to create a precedent to be followed by other debt-ridden colleges. At the time of writing, the matter remains unresolved.

Finally, the English local authority structure nationally is currently under review by the Local Government Commission for England, and a White Paper has been published on local government review in Wales. The English commission has published a number of reports for some Shire Counties, and towards the end of 1993 the government made it clear that it favoured dismantling the present structure of two-tier authorities of counties and districts and replacing with single, smaller, all-purpose authorities. In addition, some authority boundaries may well be changed and possibly some which disappeared in the previous reorganization in 1974 may be resurrected. All that can be said at this stage is that the creation of new authorities will cause the education service further dislocation at a time of major change.[29] Perhaps the further education colleges, having cut most of their links with their LEAs, with whatever attendant disadvantages, may at least count themselves fortunate in not being much affected by the impending reorganization.

The Training and Enterprise Councils (TECs)

The creation of the 82 TECs, 75 in England and 7 in Wales, and their 22 Scottish equivalents, the Local Enterprise Councils (LECs), has been described as 'arguably the most significant government policy innovation in vocational education and training in Britain in the last two decades.'[30] While potentially that may indeed have been the case, as we shall see there are good reasons to suppose that the TECs have so far failed to live up to their potential.

The decision to create the TECs was taken in the late 1980s by the then Secretary of State for Employment, Sir Norman Fowler, following a visit to the USA during which he was impressed by the TECs' American forebears, called Private Industry Councils (PICs), which had been set up as employers' organizations bringing together in local areas training enterprise and private sector investment. However, while the concept was enthusiastically embraced, no detailed evaluation was undertaken of the success or otherwise of the PICs.[31] Formally announced in the White Paper, *Employment for the 1990s*,[32] the TECs were launched in March 1989 with a formidable remit. They would be led by employers; being local bodies they would ensure that their training systems would be developed to meet local needs; as their titles indicate, they would coordinate the provision of vocational education and training in their areas; and they would be required to place greater emphasis on 'performance' and cost-effectiveness than had previously been the case. They would take over responsibility for government programmes, now primarily youth training for 16- to 19-year-olds, and training for work, for unemployed adults. Together, these two programmes accounted for four-fifths of their budget, which in 1993–94 was some £2.3 billion, supplied primarily by the government. However, as and when ED funds decrease, as seems likely, the TECs will have to generate more on their own, some from industry and some from the educational establishments. Until recently, they were also charged with responsibility for financing work-related further education (WRFE) in the colleges, the money being used to improve the responsiveness of the further education sector to the needs of both employers and individuals as well as increasing the cost-effectiveness of vocational provision. Of the WRFE money formerly at the TECs' disposal, about £100 million a year in 1994, 85 per cent was spent in accordance with the colleges' strategic plans as agreed with the funding councils and the remaining 15 per cent was used with the colleges to support the TECs' own local priorities. Now that the money is being channelled through the funding councils, the colleges are still expected to work closely with the TECs, who will have some say in the approval of further funds. In addition, the TECs are responsible for piloting the training credits scheme and for meeting the national education and training targets, no small order. Set up as private limited companies, they have a board of directors, typically 15 in number, of whom two-thirds, including the chairman, have to be local employers. One of the many quangos (quasi-autonomous national government organizations) established by the government, which approves the appointment of their chairmen, it has, in effect, a semi-private character. Members, other than those from local business and industry, usually include representatives from the local authorities, the trades unions, and the further education colleges. In order to receive funds from the TECs, the colleges and other providers of training put in bids to them to carry out their programmes. The importance to the colleges of TEC-funded programmes is such that in some colleges they provide one-third of their total budget for vocational training. Before releasing funds to the colleges, the TECs are expected to have audited their quality standards according to rigorous ED criteria. To sum up, the TECs represent a unique combination of the private and public sectors, in that the training they sponsor is the primary responsibility of employers while at the same time they draw very largely upon public funds.

In order to support the work of the individual TECs and provide them with a national voice and a pressure group, the TEC National Council was set up in July 1993 to coordinate the work of previous loose groupings of TECs. It makes major policy submissions to the government on behalf of the

TECs, publishes a range of documents, including a directory of TECs and discussion papers such as a June 1994 one on lifetime learning; facilitates and coordinates TEC discussions with other bodies such as the CBI, the TUC, and the examining and validating bodies; and supports a range of conferences on subjects of importance to TECs such as European funding and modern apprenticeships.

While the TECs deserve to be given every opportunity to achieve the formidable objectives they were set, they have been faced from the beginning with two considerable structural difficulties.[33] The first is that in some respects they are too parochial in that the geographical areas they cover are limited to counties, or parts of them, and towns and consequently they are not properly equipped to fill the vacuum in local and regional planning created by the emasculation of the local authorities and the removal from the RACs of their planning function. Secondly, because they are funded and to a considerable degree directed in policy by the government, they cannot exercise proper autonomy and make the sort of decisions best tailored to local needs. In this respect, they provide an interesting contrast with the LECs in Scotland, who have a greater degree of autonomy and, perhaps partly for this reason, are seen to be more successful.

It can also be said that the TECs were unlucky in the time of their conception: in Evans' words, 'it is their misfortune to have been conceived at a time of economic growth but launched at a time of recession'.[34] As a result, they have been overwhelmed by demands to train the unemployed, at the expense of many of their entrepreneurial activities. Moreover, they vary very greatly in size and consequently in the budgets at their disposal, and also in the character of the areas which they serve, some of which have been particularly hard hit by the recession. Thus, it was not surprising that when, in September 1993, the ED published so-called 'league tables' for the TECs, judging their performance against a range of criteria such as their success or otherwise in qualifications gained or places on recognized courses or in employment, these showed very wide variations. Even allowing for the fact that these league tables are little more than 'snapshots' of TEC activities,[35] it seems indisputable that there are great differences both between the service provided by one TEC and that provided by another and also between different programmes supported by individual TECs. When the TECs were first established, there is no doubt that many industrialists, including prominent business leaders, gave up a great deal of time and energy to serve on them and direct their endeavours. Since then, however, in many instances their interest has dwindled and indeed it was probably naive of the government to suppose that there were large numbers of industrialists with the time, commitment and ability to promote skills training on a large scale by this means. It is hardly surprising, therefore, that in some TECs there has been a rapid turnover of employers, with the result that the full-time officers, many of whom are seconded former civil servants, are effectively running them. Moreover, when first appointed to TECs many employers had little knowledge of further education and some of them were antipathetic towards its aims and ethos. Equally, many colleges were distrustful of the TECs and fearful of their intentions. In a survey conducted among the colleges by the *Times Educational Supplement* and the FEU and reported in March 1993,[36] as many as a third of the respondents said their relationships with the TECs were unproductive, with a majority of the sixth-form colleges describing them as negative or non-existent. Inevitably, there are bureaucratic difficulties, with some colleges drawing students from as many as three different TECs, each with different funding rules. The colleges have also feared, particularly in the early days of the TECs, that they would be bypassed in favour of private providers, a fear that does not generally seem to have been borne out by events. However, there is growing concern among some college principals that some TECs are running courses in direct competition with their colleges, in contravention of the terms of their contract with the ED, by which they are required to fund training by the colleges and private providers and not run their own programmes. How far this concern is justified remains unclear, as the TECs have challenged the Association for Colleges (AfC), which published a survey including claims by colleges that TECs were setting up their own training programmes, to provide firm academic evidence to substantiate these claims.

These patent shortcomings, and others, on the part of the TECs have been highlighted in an exhaustive study of their operations carried out by a group from the London School of Economics (LSE) and published in January 1994.[37] Although constructive in tone, it is nevertheless highly critical of their management and operations and among other things states that they have been deflected from their major mission of improving the skills of the workforce and stimulating business growth by being required by the government to take on 'the social problem of targeting the unemployed'. They have also come into conflict with other business-led bodies such as chambers of commerce, resulting in wasteful duplication, and to overcome this problem the report recommends that the two should be merged. Many of the TECs are considered to be too small to be cost-efficient and should be merged with others, so as to halve their present number. It is interesting to note that this view seems to be shared by the government, which in mid-1994 instructed the nine TECs covering the London area to consider reducing their numbers, possibly to as few as five. Finally, the study considers that many of the TECs have been very wasteful of public money, an accusation which, as we have seen, has led the NAO, as part of its programme of work for 1994, to decide to examine the financies of the TECs. Yet another review of the work of the TECs was conducted by the CBI in 1993 and concentrated on four aspects of their operations: their mission, their external relationships, their long-term funding, and the assessment of their performance. The results of this review were published in November 1993[38] in the form of a policy document which, while emphasizing strong support for the TECs among employers and supporting continuing funding through the tax-payers, nevertheless commented trenchantly on some of their shortcomings, including the strongly held CBI view that instead of concentrating so heavily on helping the unemployed return to work, they should devote much more time to the enterprise aspects of their mission.

These criticisms and complaints about the management and operations of the TECs inevitably raise the question of their future viability. The LSE study is quite unequivocal on the subject and forecasts that it they have not come up to scratch by 1995–96, when they have to apply for a new system of three-year licences, the government will 'pull the plug' on them. Indeed, the government's refusal to accept any responsibility for the very substantial debts incurred by the South Thames TEC before it went into receivership at the end of 1994, on the grounds that it was a private company, could be taken as an indication that the process has already started. If that happens, yet another attempt to promote industry-led training in the period since the end of World War II will have been aborted.

Other Bodies

As significant parts of the complex framework within which the further colleges operate, there are a large number of bodies which to varying degrees influence their administration and the service which they deliver. For convenience, these can be divided into four main categories. First, there are the awarding, examining and validating bodies, including the NCVQ, the Business and Technology Education Council (BTEC), the C&G and the Royal Society of Arts (RSA). While the latter three are the largest awarding bodies of certificates and diplomas at technician and craft levels, there is also a very large number of professional bodies, such as the Institute of Chartered Accountants and the Hotel, Catering and Institutional Management Association, which oversee professional awards in their respective professions and trades. Second, there are the teachers', colleges' and college employers' organizations such as the National Association of Teachers in Further and Higher Education (NATFHE), the AfC, the Association of Principals of Sixth Form Colleges (APVIC), the Colleges' Employers' Forum (CEF), and the Sixth Form Colleges' Employers' Forum. Third, there are the bodies representing industry and business such as the CBI and the TUC. And, fourth, there are the bodies concerned with staff and curriculum development, principally, at the time of writing, the FEU and the FESC. As it is not possible in a book of this kind to describe fully the work of all those bodies which, one way or another, determine and influence much of the day-to-day work of the colleges, we shall restrict ourselves to commenting upon the more important ones.

Among the best-known and most influential of the awarding, validating and examining bodies which must be mentioned are the NCVQ, BTEC, C&G and RSA. The NCVQ came into existence in October 1986, following proposals put forward in the White Paper, *Education and Training – Working Together*,[39] which appeared earlier in the same year. Formally established as an independent body, initially funded by the government, the NCVQ was given the remit of pulling together the plethora of vocational qualifications nationally available into a comprehensive and logical framework where individual qualifications relate to one another so that open access to training is facilitated and individuals can progress in a straightforward fashion from one level of qualification to another. To this end, the NCVQ introduced new forms of qualifications, or 'kitemarks', like those awarded by the British Standards' Institute (BSI), to be known as National Vocational Qualifications (NVQs). For that reason, the NCVQ is better described as a quality assurance or accrediting body, rather than an awarding body, and included in its brief was a requirement to act as a catalyst to bring the principal awarding bodies together and to monitor and assess the quality of their qualifications. The NCVQ also introduced the concept of 'levels', eventually settling on five of them, of which Level 3, for example, is defined as the equivalent of GCE A-level. These NVQ levels are applied commonly to the certificates and diplomas of all the awarding bodies as an aid to progression and transfer. The NCVQ has also devised a credit accumulation and transfer scheme which allows trainees to accumulate credit for each unit which contributes towards an NVQ so that eventually they may accumulate enough credit to be granted the award. This progression is recorded in a National Record of Vocational Achievement (NROVA) first introduced in September 1988. The criteria which the NCVQ have devised for these purposes include a shift to what it calls 'an outcome-led system of education and training', by which the requirements of qualifications are based not primarily on the content of syllabuses and training specifications, but instead on the competencies and achievements which students demonstrate as outcomes of their training.[40]

As we have seen, this 'competence-based' model has not been without its critics, who deplore the lack of rigour and understanding of underlying concepts which such a model in their view promotes. In the years since its establishment, the NCVQ has got together with the awarding bodies, notably BTEC, C&G and the RSA, industry, professional bodies and other interested parties to help it devise its assessment and verification procedures, not without, it might be added, a great deal of concern and argument on both sides. Indeed, the relationships between BTEC, for example, and the NCVQ have been very tense at times;[41] however, constructive agreements were reached until eventually, in 1991, the government decided to place BTEC, RSA and C&G qualifications under the NCVQ's exclusive control. Then, in August 1993, the NCVQ issued its document, *The Common Accord*,[42] which sets out the assessment and verification procedures relating to all its NVQ awards. This defines the roles in quality assurance for both the awarding bodies and the organizations they approve to offer them. Because of concerns expressed about the quality of NVQs across the country, the government in its May 1994 White Paper, *Competitiveness: Helping Business to Win*,[43] laid down certain requirements for local quality assurance. In response to these, the NCVQ has established a fully fledged inspectorate to monitor the delivery of NVQs by the very large number of local centres presently offering them. In addition, the Council is currently undertaking a detailed look at the NVQ system as it has developed in practice and as it is being used. In the better part of a decade since its establishment, the NCVQ has had a considerable influence on further education programmes, including more recently the introduction of the GNVQs, raising curricular issues which are examined in detail in Chapter 3.

BTEC was formed in 1983 originally as the Business and Technician Education Council, assuming its present title on 1 December 1991. For most of its existence it was a 'non-departmental public body', which meant that although it has been self-funding for years, its status was guaranteed by the Secretary of State for Education. However, in October 1993, it assumed full independence as a company linked by guarantee and a charity which exists to promote education,[44] thereby enjoying the same status as the RSA Examination Board and the C&G. Whether this change will result in greater independence from the DFE remains to be seen. The NCVQ is both a validating and examining body which designs about 300 different programmes which are mainly approved to run in colleges of further education, though some are also run 'in house' by companies and, in increasing numbers, by secondary schools. In all, throughout the UK, more than 500,000 students are enrolled on BTEC programmes which register annually more than 275,000 new students. BTEC offers three mainstream qualifications which can be taken on a full- or part-time basis from the age of 16. These are its First Certificates and Diplomas, National Certificates and Diplomas and Higher National Certificates and Diplomas, which form a progressive ladder of qualifications for students and most of which are being or have been accredited for the award of NVQs. As a validating body, BTEC encourages colleges to submit course proposals for its approval and moderation. It requires submissions to incorporate two particular features: courses must be taught by a team who meet regularly to coordinate student learning across the units which make up the course; and a student-centred approach must be adopted, including the use of case studies and integrated assignments and the deployment of a wide range of learning resources, including information technology.[45] It is scarcely surprising, therefore, that BTEC's student-centred approach to course approval should lead to conflict with the 'competence-based' and 'outcome-led' model adopted by the NCVQ, necessitating a compromise agreement. With the introduction of GNVQs, BTEC, along with C&G and the RSA, is one of the only three bodies authorized to make the award. To this end, it has been closely involved in piloting GNVQs and refining their design, and has run seminars round the country on the subject and produced a student guide. Recently, it has joined forces with C&G and the RSA to adopt a common approach to the assessment of GNVQs, including the elimination of unnecessary bureaucracy, and has agreed to a standard approach to approving GNVQ centres. It is BTEC's policy for all of its awards eventually to lead to either NVQs or GNVQs and, for this reason, many of its First and National Diploma courses are being phased out over the next few years. Finally, at the end of 1992, the government announced its intention of reviewing BTEC's constitution in order to secure future arrangements best suited to enabling it to continue to offer high-quality vocational awards and to respond effectively to the needs of students and their parents, employers, higher education, teachers and other interests. We await the outcome of this review with interest.

C&G, an autonomous body incorporated by Royal Charter in 1990, has been in existence for well over a century. It offers syllabuses in some ten major vocational areas, predominantly at craft level, and is one of the largest national examining bodies in further education. The vocational areas that attract most entrants include, in order of popularity: commerce and training; vehicles and plant maintenance; electrical and information technology; beauty and care; construction; production engineering; catering, travel and leisure; and agriculture. In addition, it has substantial numbers of students undertaking courses in general education and work preparation. Like BTEC, it is proceeding towards the position where all of its courses will lead to the award of either NVQs or GNVQs, a process to which it states it is 'wholly committed'.[46] Like BTEC, it has been closely involved with the development and implementation of both NVQs and GNVQs, into which it has put a great deal of effort; however, it comments that by 1993 at least, despite all its hard work, the take-up of these awards had been disappointing and that consequently there is a great need to promote awareness of NVQs among employers, employees and parents if the ambitious national education and training targets are to be met. It has also been much involved in developing forms of assessment for GNVQs, including portfolios of evidence to be judged by assessors, the training and accreditation of external verifiers, and the provision of external tests. Together with the eight RACs making up FEDOR, it has run numerous GNVQ workshops and training sessions.

The RSA is the oldest of the three major awarding bodies and, like the other two, provides courses for hundreds of thousands of entrants. However, its examination provision has now been hived off into a separate company, known as the RSA Examinations Board. While it makes its major provision in the fields of commercial training, English teaching and further education teacher training, in recent years it has moved into technical fields, including, for example, providing certification for courses in technology, both in colleges and schools. It has also been active in developing and implementing new NVQs in such areas as journalism and management. Like the other two major awarding bodies, it is working towards the position where all of its courses, if successfully completed, will lead to the award of an NVQ or GNVQ.

As we pointed out earlier, while BTEC, C&G and the RSA are the three largest awarding and examining bodies, there are many others whose qualifications are sought by students undertaking vocational courses in further education colleges. To name but a few, in the secretarial field are Pitmans Examinations Institution (PEI) and the London Chambers of Commerce; and in their respective fields, the National Nursery Examinations Board, the International Health and Beauty Council, and the Institute of Personnel Management.

The second group of bodies influencing further education are those organizations representing teachers, colleges, and employers. Among the organizations representing further education teachers, the largest, with some 50,000 members, and perhaps the most important, is the National Association of Teachers in Further and Higher Education (NATFHE), though as its title indicates it also represents staff in the 'new' universities, the former polytechnics. Both a trade union and a professional body, it publishes the *NATFHE Journal*, which appears three times a year, and *The Lecturer*, six times a year, two of the few publications which deal specifically, if not exclusively, with further education. In addition, from time to time it publishes policy documents and booklets on matters of current interest, including, for example, one on training credits.[47] As a trade union, it negotiates with employers on behalf of its members and, as we shall see, is currently engaged in a protracted dispute with them over salaries and working conditions. Another body, with some 4000 teachers from further education and sixth-form colleges among its members, is the Association of Teachers and Lecturers (ATL); avowedly non-party political and, unlike NATFHE, not affiliated to the TUC, it too has been involved in salary negotiations. Similarly concerned is the Association of College Managers (ACM), which is both a registered trade union and also a professional association and has some 2000 members from middle and senior management in the colleges. In the run-up to the granting of 'independence' to the further education and sixth-form colleges on 1 April 1993, two bodies came into existence representing the colleges as employers, that is their governors and principals. These are the Colleges' Employers' Forum (CEF) and the Sixth Form Colleges' Employers' Forum. The CEF, an independent body owned by the colleges with a board of directors made up of six chairs of governors and six principals, describes its main objective as the provision of relevant support and advice to the colleges on all employment matters affecting the sector as a whole. In effect, therefore, it was set up to manage industrial relations with college staffs, principally the negotiation of salaries and conditions of employment. To this end and on payment of a not inconsiderable membership fee, 355 further education colleges, which is virtually all of them, had joined the CEF by the spring of 1994. By that time, year-long negotiations with NATFHE over salaries and conditions of service had reached an impasse. Before incorporation, when staff were employed by the local authorities, these were laid down in the so-called Silver Book; however, in view of the marketplace conditions in which the colleges now find themselves, it was agreed in principle by both sides that more flexible conditions of working are now required, which means in effect longer statutory working hours per week and shorter holidays. In practice, however, the CEF and NATFHE were unable to agree on precisely what the new arrangements should be, although an agreement has been reached between the CEF and the ATL. In the meantime, the government's contribution to the impasse was to hold back 2 per cent, or £50 million, of the colleges' budgets unless and until they satisfied the funding councils that more flexible working arrangements were being introduced. This they eventually did and the money was released in mid-1994. Similar negotiations went on between the Sixth Form Colleges' Employers' Forum and the unions representing college staffs, whose circumstances are somewhat different from those in the further education colleges, as the sixth-form college staff are still tied to the School Teachers' Review Body agreements and their working contract is already a more flexible one. Nevertheless, it has been argued that without still more flexibility of staff working arrangements the sixth-form colleges will find it difficult to expand into new areas such as vocational and adult education, which they must do if they are to survive.[48]

Finally, there are three bodies representing senior managers, namely principals and governors, in further education: the Association of Principals of Colleges (APC), the AfC, and the APVIC. The APC is a long-established body which, as its title indicates, restricts its membership to college principals and represents their interests. A much more recent body is the AfC, which was launched in 1993 to campaign on behalf of further education colleges once they were removed from local authority control, and to provide curriculum development, research and other support services. It has attracted membership from the great majority of principals and governors as well as other staff, who are equally represented on its council, though a few are waiting to see what it offers. Meanwhile, it has begun to initiate research into further education by funding curriculum development projects in colleges and to undertake its own surveys, including a recent one on the provision of higher education in further education. It publishes a bi-monthly tabloid-style journal entitled *FE Now!* At one time, it seemed likely that the AfC and the APC would merge or affiliate, but at its annual conference in 1994 the latter affirmed its intention of continuing as an independent organization. The APVIC, as the title indicates, until recently restricted its membership to sixth-form college principals. However, to reflect changed managerial circumstances in the colleges it has expanded to include governors. When the AfC was originally established, it was hoped by many that the APVIC would join it to form a single body. Although this did not come about at the time, the two have worked closely together.

The third group of bodies which plays a part in the shaping of further education provision consists of those representing business and industry, of which the two most influential are the CBI and the TUC. The CBI, particularly through its education and training committee, has long played a part in further education and, as we have seen, has in recent years put forward a number of initiatives, some of which have been endorsed by the government. A good example is that of training credits, originally proposed by its Vocational Education and Training Task Force in its publication *Towards a Skills Revolution*,[49] first published in 1989. Its political influence is therefore considerable, especially with Conservative governments, and it is represented on many of the national bodies either directly or by leading employers who are members of the CBI. The TUC has also been much concerned with vocational education and training, though inevitably its political influence has declined, as has its membership, during the years of Conservative government. Indeed, the relationship between it and the government has at times been hostile, as in the late 1980s when it withdrew its support from the government's employment training scheme for unemployed adults. In the earlier part of 1994, however, the climate changed somewhat when the then Secretary of State for Employment addressed a TUC conference. Like the CBI, it has from time to time produced publications of varying degrees of influence, such as its document *Skills 2000*,[50] published in 1989, which joined with the CBI in supporting the provision of vocational qualifications of equal repute to the academic ones. It has also supported the CBI in its proposals for training credits, albeit with some reservations.

The fourth and last group of bodies affecting the provision of further education comprises those concerned with curriculum development and staff development, the two principal ones having been the FEU and the FESC. The FEU, originally known as the Further Education Curriculum

Review and Development Unit, was set up by the DES in 1977. Its remit included the review of curricula offered by further education institutions, the development of further education by carrying out specific studies, the dissemination of information on the process of curriculum development, and the promotion of quality in further education by encouraging more effective, relevant and flexible learning opportunities for individual learners. It was financed on an annual basis by the DFE until April 1993, when its funding was taken over by the funding councils. Most of its work is conducted through research and development projects and activities and, soon after its inception, the FEU rapidly established a good reputation for working closely with the colleges in developing, testing and disseminating curricular material. In the last few years, for example, it has been concerned with assisting with the production of NVQs and with the identification and development of core skills, and has published its findings in a series of bulletins on these subjects. It has also recognized that for curriculum development to succeed, college staff must be able to manage change and introduce new styles of teaching and learning, and has consequently issued a number of relevant documents on the subject. In 1992, it incorporated into itself the Unit for the Development of Adult and Continuing Education (UDACE), which has enabled it to give more attention to curriculum development in the field of adult education. Some idea of the range of its concerns may be gained from its publications catalogue, which in 1993, in addition to a major section devoted to learning programmes for 16- to 19-year-olds and for adults, included documents on guidance and participation, learners with disabilities or learning difficulties, ethnic diversity, quality and resourcing, developments in vocational education and training in Europe, and the assessment and accreditation of achievement. It also issues the quarterly *FEU Newsletter*, which usefully comments on current initiatives and developments in further education. However, as we shall see, the FEU together with the FESC will have been replaced by another body before this text is published.

The FESC, which is located at Coombe Lodge, just south of Bristol, opened in 1963. Originally jointly funded by the DES and the local authorities, it now earns two-thirds of its income through fees. It describes itself as 'The Management Development Centre for Further and Higher Education' and runs a series of 'open courses' both at Coombe Lodge and at various centres throughout the UK on such major subjects as personnel management and industrial relations, marketing, curriculum management, managing resources, and the governance of colleges, together with a series of special programmes, including one for vice-principals of colleges. In this way, it has acted as a centre for policy development by providing settings in which senior staff and others from the further education service can meet with one another as well as people from industry and elsewhere to exchange ideas, information and experiences. It offers a training and consultancy service to colleges, education authorities and other bodies, and issues a range of publications including *The Coombe Lodge Report*, published approximately monthly on subjects relevant to the management of further and higher education, *Update*, published fortnightly, a very useful review of current developments in further and higher education and vocational education and training, and the *Mendip Papers*, a series of papers written for managers in further and higher education. Over the more than 30 years of its existence, it has become generally respected by the colleges, particularly for its provision of management training.

From these brief descriptions of their activities, it can be seen that there is a degree of overlap between the work of the FEU and the FESC. Moreover, the context in which they are operating has changed considerably within the past few years. For these reasons, and doubtless others of a more political nature, the DFE asked the two FEFCs, for England and Wales, to review the role and work of the two bodies. A review group was set up for this purpose and published its report in July 1993. In the period leading up to the report, Geoff Stanton, the chief officer of the FEU, and Geoffrey Melling, the director of the FESC, had eventually come together to propose that the two bodies should merge. However, to the surprise of many in further education the review group recommended that they should be replaced by a Further Education Development Agency (FEDA). It opposed a merger partly on the not wholly convincing grounds that 'given the separate and distinct cultures of the two bodies it was thought unlikely that they could be successfully melded together'.[51] At least one knowledgeable commentator on further education matters takes issue with this recommendation, observing that while there are cultural differences between the two bodies they are not insurmountable and that further education would be better served by building on their successes and maintaining continuity during a period when the colleges need their services more than ever. However, the review group, apparently in response to views expressed by the colleges,[52] decided otherwise, believing that the new body will retain the best of its two predecessors and foster a more business-like and responsive approach. Its mission will be 'to assist the students' needs and thereby to contribute to the achievement of the national education and training targets'.[53] It will also have the important role of commissioning research into subjects of strategic importance to the further education sector. Finally, in March 1994, the DFE announced that the new developmental body would be set up on 1 April 1995 and that its remit and structure will be set by the funding councils. However, it appears that the new body's remit will also include the staff development of further education teachers, training programmes for governors and the provision of support for adult education. FEDA will have an initial budget of £7.5 million from the funding councils but this will be substantially reduced in subsequent years and it will be expected to earn money from subscriptions, fees and contracts. The chair of the new body, Ken Young, formerly chairman of the Student Loans Company, has already been appointed by the Secretaries of State for Education and Wales, who will also appoint a goodly proportion of its members. It remains to be seen how this will affect its independence and methods of working. Given the need for its services, it is to be hoped that once it comes into existence in April 1995 it gets under way quickly and efficiently.

In conclusion, it is clear that the further education sector of our educational system is a complex one, perhaps more so than any other sector, mainly because of the variety of functions it is called upon to fulfil. Thus, it offers a very wide range of opportunity geared to meet the needs of millions of people of all ages and caters for many interests. Inevitably, therefore, many controls and influences, operating at all levels, are brought to bear upon it. In a previous book, we observed that while this variety of provision is one of further education's greater glories, it does result in a degree of overlap, wastage and conflict,[54] that this was due in part to our predilection for seeking *ad hoc* solutions to specific problems rather than seeing them in the context of the system as a whole, and that there seemed little prospect that, under the pressure of events, things would change for the better. Now, looking back, we would comment rather sadly that our observation has been borne out by events.

Notes and References

1   L. M. Cantor and I. F. Roberts, *Further Education Today: A Critical Review*, London, Routledge & Kegan Paul, 1986 (3rd edn), p. 11.
2   M. Barker, '1944 and all that', *Guardian Education*, 18 January, 1994, p 2.
3   In July 1995, the Employment Department was abolished and its training functions were transferred to a new Department of Education and Employment (see also p. 155, note 1).
4   *National Advisory Council for Education and Training Targets: Report on Progress*, London, NACETT, February 1994; and *Review of the National Targets for Education and Training, Proposals for Consultation*, London, NACETT, July 1994.
5   Employment Department/Department of Trade and Industry, *Competitiveness: Helping Business to Win*, Cmnd 2563, London, HMSO, May 1994.
6   Department for Education, *Student Affairs Branch Document*, London, DFE, February 1994.
7   A. Smithers and P. Robinson, *Changing Colleges, Further Education in the Market Place*, Council for Industry and Higher Education, London, 1993.
8   Department for Education/Welsh Office, *The Charter for Further Education* and *It's Your Choice: A Guide to Choosing at 16*, London and Cardiff, DFE/Welsh Office, 1993.

9   J. McGinty and J. Fisher, *Further Education in the Market Place: Opportunity and Individual Learning*, London, Routledge, 1993.

10   B. Evans, *The Politics of the Training Market. From Manpower Services Commission to Training and Enterprise Councils*, London, Routledge, 1992, p. 177.

11   P. Raggatt and L. Unwin (eds.), *Change and Intervention: Vocational Education and Training*, London, Falmer Press, 1991, pp. 9–11.

12   S. Carrol, 'An FE Lead Body', *FEU Newsletter*, December 1993, p. 8.

13   For a detailed analysis of training credits and their introduction, see L. Unwin, 'Training credits: the pilot doomed to succeed', Chapter 9, pp. 205–223 in W. Richardson, J. Woolhouse and D. Finegold (eds), *The Reform of Post-16 Education and Training in England and Wales*, London, Longman, 1993.

14   J. Croall, 'Pathfinders who have lost their way', *Guardian Supplement*: 'Skills for the Future', 3 March 1994, p. 4; and 'Raring to Go – New Style Careers Service Ready to Take Off', *Insight*, No. 29, Spring 1994, pp. 19–21.

15   Employment Department/Department of Trade and Industry, *Competitiveness: Helping Business to Win, op. cit.*

16   M. Chapman, 'In my view', *Insight*, No. 29, Spring 1994, p. 3.

17   National Foundation for Educational Research, *Evaluation of Second Year of Training Credits*, Slough, NFER, 1993.

18   Audit Commission, *Obtaining Better Value from Further Education*, London, Audit Commission, 1985.

19   I. McNay, 'Cooperation, coordination and quality in employer and education partnerships: a role for the regions', p. 98 in P. Raggatt and L. Unwin (eds), *Change and Intervention: Vocational Education and Training*, London, Falmer Press, 1991.

20   Audit Commission, *Unfinished Business: Full-time Educational Courses for 16–19 year olds*, London, Audit Commission, 1993.

21   J. Short, 'How will colleges manage', *Times Higher Education Supplement*, 10 December 1993, p. 23.

22   The Further Education Funding Council, *Funding Learning*, Coventry, FEFC, December 1992.

23   T. Tysome, 'Putting a price – and a value – on FE', *Times Higher Education Supplement*, 16 July 1993, p. 6.

24   J. Short, *op. cit.*

25   The Further Education Funding Council, *Assessing Achievement*, Coventry, FEFC, April 1993.

26   T. Melia, 'When the inspectors start to call', *Times Higher Education Supplement*, 26 March 1993, p. viii.

27   The Further Education Funding Council for Wales, *Funding FE in Wales*, Cardiff, FEFCW, September 1993.

28   L. South, 'The LASER Advisory Council', *BTEC Briefing*, **14**, 12 (1994).

29   J. Williams, 'Border skirmishes', *Times Educational Supplement*, 10 December 1993, p. 15.

30   M. Maguire, 'Training Enterprise Councils', Chapter 8 in T. Whiteside, A. Sutton and T. Everton (eds), *16–19, Changes in Education and Training*, London, David Fulton, 1992, p. 95.

31   P. Ryan (ed.), *International Comparisons of Vocational Education and Training for Intermediate Skills*, London, Falmer Press, 1991, p. 25.

32   Employment Department, White Paper, *Employment for the 1990s*, Cmnd 540, London, HMSO, 1989.

33 B. Evans, *The Politics of the Training Market. From Manpower Services Commission to Training and Enterprise Councils*, London, Routledge, 1992, p. 226.

34 *Ibid.*

35 T. Tysome, 'Snapshot of TECs shows blurred edges', *Times Higher Education Supplement*, 17 September 1993, p. 3.

36 T. Tysome, 'Marriage strains', *Times Higher Education Supplement*, Synthesis/Further Education, 26 March 1993, p. xi.

37 R. J. Bennett, P. Wicks and A. McCoshan, *Local Empowerment and Business Services: Britain's Experiment with TECs,* London, UCL Press, 1994.

38 Confederation of British Industry, *Making Labour Markets Work, London*, CBI Publications, London, 1993.

39 Employment Department/Department of Education and Science, White Paper, *Education and Training – Working Together*, Cmnd 9823, London, HMSO, 1986.

40 For a detailed account of NCVQ and its workings, see G. Jessup, *Outcomes: NVQs and the Emerging Model of Education and Training*, London, Falmer Press, 1991. See also J. Burke (ed.), *Competency Based Education and Training*, London, The Falmer Press, 1989.

41 K. Spours, 'Analyses: The reform of qualifications within a divided system', p. 162 in W. Richardson, J. Woolhouse and D. Finegold (eds), *The Reform of Post-16 Education and Training in England and Wales*, London, Longman, 1993.

42 National Council for Vocational Qualifications, *The Common Accord*, London, NCVQ, August 1993.

43 Employment Department/Department of Trade and Industry, *Competitiveness: Helping Business to Win*, op. cit.

44 E. Fennell, 'Cut loose from nanny's apron strings', *Times Supplement*, BTEC At Work, 4 October 1993, p. iv.

45 P. Mayre, 'Teaching and learning styles', p. 72 in T. Whiteside, A. Sutton and T. Everton (eds), *16–19, Changes in Education and Training*, London, David Fulton, 1992.p

46 City and Guilds of London Institute, *Pathways to Progress*, Annual Report 1992–93, London, CGLI, 1994, p. 4.

47 Youthaid NATFHE, *Credit Limit – A Critical Assessment of the Training Credit Pilot Scheme*, London, NATFHE, 1993.

48 I. Nash, 'Sixth form prospects poor but peaceful', *Times Educational Supplement*, 18 February 1994, p. 9.

49 Confederation of British Industry, *Towards a Skills Revolution, Report of the Vocational Education and Training Task Force*, London, CBI, October 1989.

50 Trades Union Congress, *Skills 2000*, London, TUC, 1989.

51 'Development Agency for FE', *EDUCA*, September 1993, p. 7.

52 P. Santinelli, 'FE Unit merger reflected', *Times Higher Education Supplement*, 6 August 1993, p. 2.

53 EDUCA, 'A Development Agency for FE', *EDUCA, op. cit.*

54 L. M. Cantor and I. F. Roberts, *Further Education Today: A Critical Review*, London, Routledge & Kegan Paul, 1986 (3rd edn), p. 37.

Three

Curricula in Further Education

If by 'curriculum' is meant that selection of skills, knowledge and experiences which is planned in order for students to learn, there is no single curriculum specification for further education to mirror the National Curriculum in the schools, and nor could there be. The diversity of aims of the courses found in further education, and the variety of objectives of those studying them, have presented substantial obstacles to those who have tried to create study experiences which have common elements for students throughout the sector. For 16- to 19-year-olds, for instance, it is arguable that their educational experience should include the opportunity to develop certain personal and intellectual abilities, no matter what the focus of their study. This debate, about what have come to be called 'core skills,'[1] will be examined further in this chapter; these do not, however, constitute a National Curriculum.

Curriculum design in further education is largely determined by the major examining and validating bodies. These are mostly legally independent of government and operate on a commercial basis. Their relationship with each other is therefore competitive and they are not easily influenced by government policy, although there have been some significant shifts in their practice in the last few years. The main and best known providers of vocational qualifications are the Business and Technology Education Council (BTEC), City and Guilds (C&G) and the Royal Society of Arts (RSA). In addition, there are over 200 other examining boards, most of them associated with the professional bodies which are responsible for standards in a particular area of work. They are gradually bringing their examining arrangements into line with the framework established by the National Council for Vocational Qualifications (NCVQ), in an attempt to create some coherence in this varied scene, often described as a 'jungle'[2] in the early 1980s. In addition to the vocational courses controlled by these bodies, further education colleges offer academic or non-vocational courses; indeed, just over half of all A-level GCE entries are from students in further education. The arrangements for these courses are comparable to those in schools, although the candidates may differ greatly in age, educational background, and aspiration. The GCE examining boards also oversee the examining arrangements for students in further education who are taking the examinations of the General Certificate of Secondary Education (GCSE), often for the second or third time, after failure at secondary school. The success rate of these students is generally poor, with a 30 per cent pass rate not unusual, and in the last decade there have been consistent attempts to provide alternatives for this group of students which would offer them a greater chance of success, and better motivation.

The main curriculum categories are those mentioned in Chapter 1. They are academic, occupationally specific, general vocational, and recreational. Firstly, there is provision for those whose aims are primarily academic, who may not have decided on a career path, who probably have some form of higher education study in view, and for whom the curriculum is based on the assumed demands of those higher education courses and the preparation needed for further study. This provision is mainly A-level GCE, and the less common AS (Advanced Supplementary) examination, offered as a way of broadening the usual three-subject A-level course. Secondly, there is provision which is closely linked to the training requirements of particular jobs, and courses which may be designed to support learning at work. With the establishment of the NCVQ in 1986, the basis for the design of work-based learning has radically altered, and will be discussed later in this chapter.

However, the curriculum category which has developed most rapidly in the last decade has been the third: that provision which has a vocational slant, but for which the aims are still predominantly those of a general education, for example the General National Vocational Qualification (GNVQ), or Vocational A-level, as it is alternatively named. This model is most often designed for full-time students aged 16 to 19 who do not wish to follow a course based on single academic subjects, such as GCSE or A-level, or for older people, often unemployed or changing jobs, who feel the need to develop some abilities not strictly required for particular jobs, in order to maintain flexibility in the workplace. The model has also been successfully adapted for students with learning difficulties, increasing numbers of whom have been provided for by further education colleges in the last 15 years, as local education authorities (LEAs) altered their policies on the education of those aged 16 and over who had special needs. Courses offering training for the unemployed have been subject to some of the most rapid changes in the last few years, as the government has introduced successive schemes in an attempt to respond to the varying needs created by the economic recession. Colleges have not always been part of these schemes, but where they have participated they have been able to create some ingenious mixes of basic educational skills, job-specific training, enterprise skills, and personal development, all offered on a flexible basis to respond to the needs of a very volatile group of students.

Courses which are purely recreational in purpose have been removed by the 1992 Further and Higher Education Act from the scope of further education. During the passing of the legislation there was vociferous debate in the adult education sector about what constituted such a definition of purpose. It is clear that the motivations of mature learners do not follow neatly the broad categories outlined above. Some may take a welding course out of general interest and to pursue a hobby and may even, through personal pride, take an end-of-course examination. Others may take creative courses out of general interest, for instance in cake decorating, and turn the experience into a successful career. It is not unusual to find adults following part-time courses as a kind of therapy, following breakdown or bereavement. In any one class, therefore, there will be a mixture of motivations, so that a teacher cannot take for granted the assumptions about student need which underpin the curriculum design of a particular course as it is prescribed by an examining board. For instance, the assumption that all students learning a vocationally relevant skill will have the opportunity to practise it in the workplace is misplaced. Adult educators have to take account of this by providing extra opportunities for practice, and special arrangements for assessment to meet the requirements of the NCVQ.

For some time this has been true of many vocational courses. The traditional basis of further education was the provision of part-time courses to accompany experience gained in the workplace by an apprentice, trainee technician, or the practitioners of trades and professions. The assumption behind the design of these courses was that the student was employed in the field of study, and was supplementing and complementing his or her – almost always his – practical experience, in study during time when he was released from work. This form of study was, and is, most commonly referred to as 'day release'. For those not fortunate to be granted time off by their employers to study, there were also evening-only versions of most of the courses, in a tradition going back to the mechanics institutes of the nineteenth century. Professional progression would be tied to success in the course examinations.

As the recession of the early 1980s increased the demand for full-time courses and special training schemes for the unemployed, course designers responded by providing full-time variants of the old part-time courses, often carrying the same qualifications. Examples of provision which expanded quickly were the full-time catering courses, leading to the same C&G qualifications as the part-time courses, but with practical experience provided in a training restaurant in the college, rather than the workplace. As the number of students who were not employed expanded, it became apparent that their success was hampered by the absence of prolonged practical experience in the workplace. Full-time students could sometimes be provided with short periods of work experience in the industry but as the rate of industrial change, and in some cases collapse, quickened, colleges were increasingly forced to simulate workplace experiences in their own workshops, practice offices, training restaurants, and the like. In some respects, this worked well. One of the criticisms of the old day-release model was that there was insufficient linkage between experience gained in the workplace and what was taught at college. There were some very outmoded practices enshrined in the syllabuses of some courses, despite their scrutiny by committees of practitioners convened by the examining bodies. Students attending colleges full-time could benefit from well-integrated programmes of theory and practice, the latter including work experience which was planned to complement the remainder of the programme.

For many reasons, however, this ideal was difficult to achieve. The liaison between colleges and industry was not always very close. In this respect, trainees in the UK are often at a marked disadvantage compared to those elsewhere in western Europe, where vocational training, even for full-time students, is well supported by industry, with advice and funds. College equipment was rarely as good as the most modern in industrial use and work experience was not always easy to arrange, especially where the industry itself was in decline. Some colleges ran full-time courses as a way of retaining staff and facilities when the industry which would provide jobs for the students had all but disappeared. For example, opportunities for qualified motor vehicle mechanics declined as motor car dealers ran their own training programmes based on the requirements for servicing their own makes of car. As a result, young people graduating from full-time motor vehicle courses found it exceptionally difficult to find work, except in small garages operating at the bottom end of the business, or in specialist workshops dealing with classic cars or agricultural machinery. The high turnover of workers in some industries concealed the fact that colleges were turning out from their full-time courses more qualified people than could reasonably be absorbed by the available jobs. Hairdressing is an example of the over-supply of qualified people, with a number equal to one-fifth of the employed workforce studying for qualifications at any one time. Since it is not possible for such a proportion to obtain adequate practical experience in 'real' work, it follows that many qualification holders would have obtained the same paper qualification as past craftspeople would have done, but with a fraction of their practical experience. On the whole, the qualification was associated with job-related knowledge and understanding, tested under examination conditions, rather than job competence. In the engineering industry, trainees were required to complete a record of certain practical tasks undertaken to a given standard, as well as to pass their written and theoretical examinations, but even employed trainees spent nearly a whole year in training away from the workplace, in order to acquire this basic competence.

Where opportunities for training in employment had declined, young people were offered job-related training through the Youth Training Scheme (YTS), or variants of it which were offered as successive modifications of the original programme, begun in 1981, following the publication of the Manpower Services Commission's (MSC) consultative paper, *A New Training Initiative: An Agenda for Action*.[3] YTS was primarily designed to offer training to those who would otherwise have been unemployed, although the same criteria in programme design were intended to apply to employed young people in company training programmes or apprenticeships. These initiatives provided a further challenge to curriculum designers, because the number of occupations for which training was sought rose dramatically and colleges were asked to supply related training in areas where they had no existing expertise and in which a qualification structure was not readily available. Retailing, information technology, bicycle repairs, saddlery and small animal husbandry are examples of training schemes for which young people sought related off-the-job training. The difficulty that colleges found in responding to some of these diverse demands led both to the search for curricula based on 'generic skills', and also to a move by some employers to take greater responsibility for training in the workplace. Generic skills were those abilities which it was assumed would be of use in a wide range of occupations, such as good communications, skill in the use of information technology and problem-solving. With a good grounding in these skills, it was believed that job-specific skills could be readily learned at work, and that transfer between occupations could be made successfully in an unstable job market.[4] The need to give credit for work-based training was a factor in the creation of the policies of the NCVQ. As we have seen, the NCVQ was established in October 1986, following proposals put forward in the White Paper, *Working Together – Education and Training*,[5] which had been published earlier in that year. The NCVQ's remit was to reform the structure of vocational qualifications in England and Wales and to increase dramatically the proportion of the population holding work-related qualifications. The NCVQ was to be responsible for bringing the qualified workforce closer to the level of competence found in other western European countries and among other international competitors, notably in the Far East. While this body is likely to prove to be the most influential agent for change in the further education curriculum organization during the present decade, the battle for dominance in both commercial and curriculum terms between the NCVQ, the established examining and validating bodies and the further education colleges themselves is still joined, with some professional bodies acting both as cheerleaders and '*agents provocateurs*'. The major tension in curriculum design is between the need to meet the learning needs of a particular student and the assumed requirements of a particular occupation.

The remainder of this chapter is a guide to the main institutions which have influenced the further education curriculum through the 1980s and early 1990s. By 'curriculum' is meant that selection of knowledge, skills and experiences which is planned for students. The power to determine the overall shape of this provision for a group of students is ultimately retained in the hands of teachers and college managers, in contrast to the school curriculum, which has been determined by law since the Education Reform Act 1988. In practice, the detail of the curriculum in further education is determined by the course and examination objectives set by examining bodies in their syllabuses, or agreed between colleges and a validating body such as BTEC. BTEC's practice has been to offer colleges the opportunity to design their own courses, in conjunction with their industry partners, and to 'validate' or approve these local designs. However, it has become more common for colleges to base their courses on standard units or modules approved in advance by BTEC, although local variations are still possible. Under the terms of the 1988 Act, the Secretary of State retains the power, which is slowly being exercised, to allow only certain further education courses and examinations from an approved list to be funded. This will impose a further restriction on locally designed courses run outside the scope of the major examining bodies, although there is still room to shape the selection of experiences which students may have as part of their formal programme, for instance by varying the style and amount of teaching, or by adding elements such as sports, community service, and other activities complementary to the main study. The funding councils' funding regime will, of course, have a gradual effect on what the colleges offer, as will the incentives offered by the TECs to run programmes approved by the NCVQ.

As the range of full-time courses in colleges grew in the 1980s, encouraged by the relatively generous funding associated with full-time students as compared to part-time, many colleges experimented with ways of creating an educational experience for their students which rivalled what it was assumed was offered in the best school sixth forms or sixth-form colleges. For many years, colleges had tried to broaden the experience of their part-time students with a programme of general studies, with greater or lesser success. For full-time students, these programmes were more elaborate, with tutorial group sessions, careers guidance, and an often impressive range of extracurricular activities, particularly in the tertiary colleges, which had inherited from the school sixth forms which they had absorbed a positive pastoral and recreational tradition. In many places, the competition between colleges and schools for students encouraged these developments, as colleges felt compelled to offer those opportunities which were promoted by schools as a benefit of staying on in the sixth form. The greater concern with the 'whole educational experience', as compared with the part-time day-release course, led to some interesting and often expensive experiments with personal and social education. Tutorial sessions provide one example, although there is little evidence that these have been used to full effect. Nevertheless, a tutorial system is an important opportunity for students to obtain some personal attention from a person designated to keep an eye on their overall progress.

The Unified Vocational Preparation (UVP) scheme,[6] which was terminated in 1983, and some of the early youth training schemes, had demonstrated the benefits to many young people of periods of residential education, and some colleges expended considerable energy and resources in offering these experiences to as many as possible of their full-time students. While GCE A-level geography students had generally had the benefit of a field trip, they were now joined by language students on exchange trips with European partners, tourism students completing projects on the Costa del Sol, catering students running hotels by the sea for a week, and many others participating in outdoor pursuits training or inner city community work for their character-building properties. This type of experience, which the colleges felt enhanced the young people's personal development, clearly brings some important new factors into the further education curriculum. If the mainstay of the college is working with a student full-time, rather than with one whom an employer sends for training on one day per week, then it follows that colleges will be persuaded to include other elements in a curriculum which are of benefit to the full-time student.

Another example of the way in which colleges help individual students is the provision of learning support, usually through some kind of open-access 'clinic' for students referred by specialist tutors as needing help with their studies. Several factors contributed to the appearance and effectiveness of learning support services. A major one was the creation of opportunities for young people with special educational needs, which grew very quickly from around 1980, following the publication of the 1978 Warnock Report on the education of children and young people with special needs. The Education Act of 1981, which encouraged the greater integration of students with learning difficulties and disabilities into mainstream education, also accelerated the shift of provision for such students over the age of 16 into further education colleges from special schools. There were sound educational as well as financial reasons for this, and most colleges embraced their new responsibilities by trying to provide an appropriate curriculum and also to equip teaching staff with some new skills. Social and life skills training, and some sheltered work experience, formed the normal basis for these courses, as well as a continuation of basic educational activity.[7]

At the same time, some of the former general studies programmes, especially for part-time students, were finally replaced by more structured programmes of study based on the development of communication and study skills. These two factors produced a group of staff who could reasonably be charged with the task of providing a general 'learning support' service, which ranged from adult literacy provision, to essay-writing help for GCE A-level students, through help for students suffering from dyslexia.

A major boost to the provision of opportunities to study beyond the immediate aims of the academic subject or vocational area was given by the Technical and Vocational Education Initiative (TVEI). This major and influential programme of curriculum change was generously funded by the Employment Department (ED), at first from 1983 through the MSC, then the Training Agency (TA) and latterly from 1990 through the ED's Training, Education and Enterprise Directorate (TEED). As its aim was to increase the relevance of the school curriculum to working life in industry and commerce, the bulk of the resources available went into schools, directed at students from 14 to 18 years of age. As the pilot programmes proceeded up the age range, however, and the programme was extended to every LEA which wished to participate, colleges inevitably became involved as major providers of technical expertise and vocational training experience. The first link with TVEI programmes for colleges was usually the provision of job-related work for school students in the 14 to 16 age range. It was expected, however, that colleges would be represented on planning and steering groups for local initiatives, and they were by this means drawn into the design of the general objectives for the programmes. Most TVEI contracts were drawn up in terms of student 'entitlements', which were no less important for 16- to 19-year-olds than for younger students. These varied from LEA to LEA, but generally included some careers guidance, personal and social education, training in information technology, work experience, a commitment to equal opportunities, and the opportunity to learn a modern foreign language. When they were introduced into further education colleges these entitlements prompted some important innovations. Meanwhile, some colleges had already arrived at the same point, travelling from another direction.

In 1979, the Further Education Unit (FEU) had published its important report, *A Basis for Choice* (ABC). Following a review of the many and varied courses available to 17-year-olds and the uses which were made of them, the report suggested the development of a unifying core of study experience to create some common ground among the courses on offer. The debates and developments following ABC[8] were long and complex and, among other things, induced political and commercial tensions between the providers of one-year courses. The tension was strongest between the providers of vocational courses and the advocates of the Certificate of Extended Education (CEE), a one-year, single-subject academic course offered mainly in schools, in the year between Ordinary- and Advanced-level GCE examinations. In due course, the government took the bold step of abandoning the CEE and asked the C&G to establish a completely new course of vocational preparation. This course was subsequently subsumed into the Certificate of Pre-Vocational Education (CPVE), run jointly by C&G and BTEC. The joint board established to oversee CPVE was eventually disbanded, and C&G was given the responsibility of running a new, improved course, called the Diploma of Vocational Education. Eventually, as we shall see later, the GNVQ appeared on the scene. All these courses, or study programmes, had in common the idea of continuing general education within the context of vocational study, as a preparation for adult and working life. They represent variations, often politically determined because of the difficult relationship between the ED and DFE, on the idea of 'vocational preparation'.

What these many twists and turns never accomplished, however, was a rationalization of the many courses on offer to 16- and 17-year-olds. At best, the notion of a core of desirable experiences was adopted by curriculum designers, and the TVEI 'entitlements' owe much to the thinking to be found in ABC, together with its background research. ABC's common core included communication skills, numeracy, information technology, social, economic and industrial awareness, moral and aesthetic education, and opportunities for personal growth and development. For the vast majority of students and staff, however, the prime reason for students attending further education colleges was to increase their job-related skills and knowledge or to pass examinations which would enhance their future career prospects. Personal development, generic skills, core curricula, and so on, were important, but only insofar as they prepared young people to jump the hurdle into work or higher education. When the effectiveness of colleges is judged by such bodies as the National Audit Office (NAO), or the Further Education Funding Councils (FEFCs), quantitative measures, or 'performance indicators', are used. One of the most influential of these is the success of students, defined in terms of examination passes and qualifications gained, or progress into further and higher education. The students themselves have very specific targets as far as the acquisition of qualifications is concerned, so that a continuing difficulty with the development of core and common skills was that while they contributed to the progress and examination success of students, they did not determine their success. Knowledge which is not amenable to formal assessment has not been accorded such high status as that which is. The introduction of GNVQs has attempted to tackle this problem in ways which are described later in the chapter.

These hurdles are still maintained and guarded by the same set of examining and validating bodies which in one form or another have controlled the further education curriculum and its quality for over 100 years. The three most widespread and important of these are the RSA, C&G and BTEC. The oldest of these is the Royal Society for the Encouragements of Arts, Manufactures and Commerce, founded by Prince Albert, and commonly known as the Royal Society of Arts, which has now hived off its examinations business into a separate company and literally sent it to Coventry. It continues to be profitable, and makes its major provision in the fields of commercial training, English teaching, and further education teacher training, although it has had some success in rivalling C&G in some more technical fields. Its main business is still in single-subject examinations, although it has developed some integrated courses, for which the assessment arrangements are more varied, with a mix of coursework, teacher assessments, and examinations.

C&G or the City and Guilds of London Institute as it was known until quite recently, was established in 1812. It has an unrivalled position in craft and technical examining, although it has diversified into practically all the areas of training which are to be found in further education, and its fastest growing qualification in 1992 was the Further Education Teachers' Certificate. As an examining body it makes judgements, by examination of the outcomes, or results of the education or training process, but does not seek to have too much influence on the process itself. How things are taught is a professional matter for its approved examination centres. It sets its syllabuses in consultation with committees from the professions and trades that it serves, and then assesses the achievements of students. Its examiners visit colleges and schools which are approved centres, and may be critical of inadequate resources. It has developed some courses, notably in the area of vocational preparation, where teacher assessment plays a larger part than formal examinations. In recent years, it has created a local presence for its centres by entering into agreements with some of the regional advisory councils for further education (RACs), such as the Yorkshire and Humberside Association for Further and Higher Education and the East Midlands Further Education Council, which, as we have seen in the previous chapter, also act as examinations boards in their own right. Whether such agreements make much difference to the curricular offerings of colleges is debatable, but they do have the advantage of a degree of local control over the assessment of the curriculum which has been particularly important in the past in the North and Midlands. For instance, at the same time as the UVP programme was nationally designed to meet the needs of young people in operative-level jobs who had traditionally not been offered qualifications, the Trades Education Courses (TRADEC) scheme, with the same aims, was established in Yorkshire as a local initiative by colleges, employers, and the regional examining board. The impact of the NCVQ on the work of C&G and RSA is discussed later.

By contrast BTEC is a validating body. This means that it approves a package of arrangements in a given centre for the design, teaching, resourcing and assessment of courses. Thus, it concerns itself with the process of running the courses, and not just their outcomes, tested in the form of examinations. Consequently, the nature of its relationship with its centres is quite different from that of the examining bodies. Colleges and schools which wish to offer its courses must submit a course application to BTEC, demonstrating in detail how the general requirements it lays down will be met. This 'submission' explains how the course will be run, with details of study content, assessments, and the resources to be made available, including the teaching expertise. There is also a requirement to show how the course relates to the needs of local industry, with the implication that employers should be consulted on matters of course design and marketing. BTEC's concern is therefore more specifically with matters of process. While it lays down general guidelines about the design framework for its 'products', some of them are quite specific, such as the requirement for BTEC courses to contain training in 'common skills'. These include information technology, communications, number skills, and the ability to solve problems and to work productively with other people. Its assessment and quality assurance arrangements consist of the provision of moderators, responsible to chief assessors, who examine the work of centres in an attempt to ensure comparable standards across institutions. The task of assessment, however, is in the hands of the centres themselves. Most programmes do not involve formal examinations, but base their assessment on student coursework and set assignments. BTEC has invested considerable energy and funds in training the staff in its centres and in schools and colleges in the various aspects of its work, and its requirements have led to a growth in confidence among these staff about course design and assessment issues, with some imaginative teamwork being applied to the design of student assignments, particularly those which combine work from the various course disciplines. These interdisciplinary, 'cross-modular' arrangements and their integrative assignments have been an important feature of BTEC's philosophy, producing, it is believed, a broad understanding among students of the field of study and a greater capacity to transfer their learning from one context to another. BTEC has offered its awards at several levels. The General, later First, awards were originally the base level, for those leaving school with very modest attainments; however, a Foundation award has been added, mainly for those in the final year of school, or those who could not, because of their other studies, obtain a full Certificate or Diploma. The National award, now aligned with NCVQ Level 3, is normally obtained after two years of post-16 study and can lead to entry into a course of higher education. The Higher National award is BTEC's higher education level qualification and overlaps the first one or two years of degree-level work found in vocational courses in universities.

Apart from students studying for the awards of these three major bodies and the satellite organizations represented by the RACs and their examination bodies, there are students in further education who are studying for qualifications which are controlled by a myriad of professional bodies, while outside the formal system, in private tutorial and correspondence colleges, the range is even greater. For example, there are courses controlled by the Department of Transport, for heavy goods vehicle and fork-lift truck driving, others offered by the Pitmans Examinations Institute (PEI), the Institute of Bankers, the Health and Safety Executive, the Institute of Embalmers, and literally hundreds more.

In 1986, as a result of government policy foreshadowed in the White Paper, *Working Together – Education and Training*,[9] into this richly, some would say chaotically, varied situation, came the NCVQ. There were various overt objectives for the NCVQ which were set by government, and a number of more covert ones. Its main aim was to achieve some rationalization of the tangle of vocational qualifications already described, by creating a framework of vocational areas and levels of achievement within them into which existing qualifications would fit. It was not intended that the NCVQ would itself become an examining body and it was described as a 'kitemarking' organization, overseeing and setting the standards of qualifications offered by others. The 'kitemark' is the sign used by the British Standards Institute (BSI) to indicate that a given product meets its standards, and the NCVQ used the term to describe its role as an accrediting or quality assurance body. Included in its brief was a requirement to act as a catalyst to bring the principal awarding bodies together and to monitor and assess the quality of their qualifications. By ensuring that all occupational groups were provided with a coherent qualification structure, it was intended to increase the opportunities available to employed people to obtain qualifications in their field of employment. As we have seen, the occupational groups were to be represented by industry lead bodies drawn from, or specially constituted by, the relevant sectors of industry. The ED then established the National Training Task Force, a mainly consultative group which was given the task of setting 'national education and training targets'. As we have seen, these are ambitious in that it is intended, for example, that within a five-year period 80 per cent of the employed workforce will have qualifications available to them, and that by 1996 50 per cent of the workforce will be aiming for National Vocational Qualifications (NVQs) or units contributing towards them. The provision of these qualifications will be designed to suit existing skill levels and not necessarily to improve them. When comparing skill levels of the workforce in the UK with those of industrial competitors it is not clear whether UK workers fall behind in their actual levels of skill or in their possession of qualifications.

Hence, the recognition and certification of existing levels of skill as a foundation for progression were an essential starting point in the NCVQ's policy. It did not assume that further education colleges were natural providers of training, nor did it seek to take on board, at least initially, the existing qualifications offered by the main examining and validating bodies.

The NCVQ could have taken the easy way out and set a framework into which existing qualifications could have fitted, ascribing to them levels which would gradually have led to comparable standards being recognized across disciplines and employment sectors. Instead, it took a much more radical approach. Five levels were set, with Level 1 being the most basic for those working under close supervision, Level 2 being the basic craft or intermediate level, Level 3 being the advanced craft or technician level and equivalent to 2 GCE A-levels, Level 4 being the higher technician and management level, and Level 5 being the professional level (Figure 3.1). The industry lead bodies were invited to set out the standards of competence for employees in their industries, mainly starting with Levels 2 and 3. These standards were to be expressed as 'can do' statements and the criteria for the performance of the competence to the required level were also to be set. Illustrations of the context in which the competence might be judged were also required – these are known as range statements. This was a mammoth undertaking for which many employment sector groups were ill-equipped and, indeed, there were no obviously representative groups for some significant sectors. In some industries such as printing, the motor trades, and electrical installation, the various professional groups were reluctant to combine and, when they did, other groups within their industries refused to recognize them. Many of these trades had strong allegiances to guilds and societies which were already guardians of their standards and, in some cases, entry to the profession. Some of these guilds, in their turn, had traditional links with C&G, through whose examinations the guild members or other professional practitioners influenced standards. Among these professional practitioners were many further education college lecturers. For this and other reasons, there were real dangers that the 'skills revolution' might founder on thinking that was old, rather than new. The industrial training boards, set up to control the quality and quantity of industrial training, had almost all been disbanded, but some of their former members and their ways of thought were still influential in the field of industrial training, and among the new industrial lead bodies.

The stage was thus set for some battles royal, with the control of further education curricula, and even the survival of colleges, as issues to be resolved. A key feature of the NCVQ philosophy[10] was that it did not matter how knowledge and skills were acquired, as long as appropriate

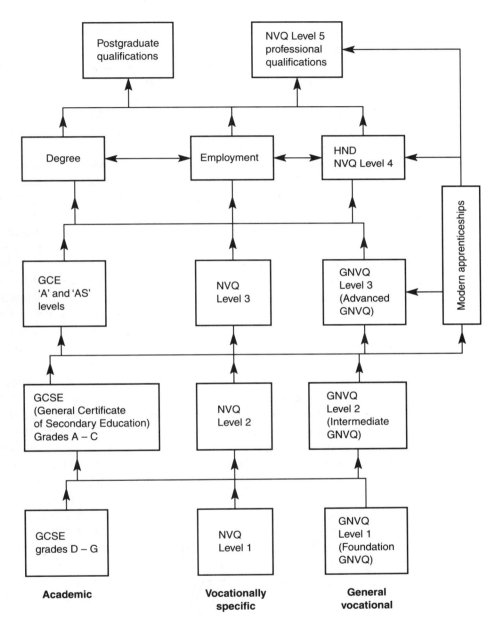

Figure 3.1: *The Major Categories of Awards: Progression Through Qualifications*
(Source: William Hall, *Vocational Education of 15–19 Year Olds: Australia and England Compared,* National Centre for Vocational Education Research, Australia, p. 25)

standards of performance could be demonstrated – only outcomes were important. While many employed people were already competent, they did not carry any form of certification of this competence. However, under the new dispensation, if their employers, or some other approved person, would assess the evidence they might offer of this competence, they could, through an approved awarding body, be awarded an NVQ at an appropriate level. There is a credit accumulation and transfer scheme which allows trainees to accumulate credit for each unit comprising an NVQ and this progression is recorded in a National Record of Vocational Achievement (NROVA), first introduced in September 1988.

At first, it was asserted by the NCVQ that the only evidence which would be acceptable for an NVQ would be assessment in the workplace. This constituted a threat to colleges as it might no longer be necessary for those wanting qualifications to attend courses. If competence could only be demonstrated in the workplace, this immediately put in jeopardy all college-based full-time courses, unless they included significant periods of work experience. After a period of intense lobbying by those in further education, and some fears that the NCVQ's own targets might not be met, it was accepted by the NCVQ that simulated work experience, for instance in the college training restaurant or motor vehicle workshop, would be acceptable. This, too, had significant implications for further education college curricula. Some of the questions it raised included: what place would there be for the theoretical knowledge which made up significant proportions of the college courses, how could students be given the necessary background and skills to provide the foundation upon which competent performance would be built, and what would happen to the carefully constructed, well-established programmes offered through BTEC, where the curriculum rationale was the integration of learning, not the assessment of minute and separated skill elements? This last question sparked off a debate which was particularly ironic; BTEC had been formed in 1983 from a merger of the Business Education Council (BEC) and the Technician Education Council, and the years after the merger were spent resolving the tension between the conflicting curriculum traditions of the two organizations. The Technician Education Council had its course specifications drawn up as a series of objectives to be met and individually assessed, usually by formal tests, so that in many ways it was an industrial training model in the same tradition as that which was now proposed by the NCVQ. The difference with the Technician Education Council was that the latter's courses were generally intended to consist of the theoretical understanding which was complementary to work-based training, and this was not always specifically assessed. The BEC tradition was quite different, being based on the thesis that in order to operate effectively a successful business employee needed an understanding of the whole organization and business in which he or she worked. Skills development, while necessary, would be fitted into the context of both personal development and the understanding of the organization. BTEC's policy of common skills and integrated course design as a foundation for specific job skills represented the partial victory of the BEC curriculum model over that of the Technician Education Council. It was never a complete victory, since college control of course submissions allowed some of the traditional Technician Education Council elements of course delivery to remain in place. However, for those who had been participants in this particular debate, the NCVQ's policy of specifying outcomes only in competence terms and distancing itself from the learning process seemed a retrograde and most undesirable development. More recently, the development of NVQs has been subjected to fierce criticism, especially by comparison with European standards, by researchers at the Manchester University Centre for Education and Employment Research. Their report, *All our Futures*,[11] which was featured in a Channel 4 'Dispatches' programme, gave a public airing to many of the concerns about the standards and philosophies of the NCVQ which have been expressed by insiders. These concerns include: doubts about the interpretation of standards by trainers, assessors and verifiers; the linking of funding to outcomes, whereby teachers have a vested interest in getting students through qualifications which they themselves assess; and a general absence of required theoretical learning to support good practice.

These are serious criticisms which were vigorously challenged by the NCVQ. Nevertheless, unease remains that the competence-based approach leaves out some important learning activity related to underpinning knowledge with experience and understanding. This unease is evidenced by the continuing resistance to the NCVQ's philosophies by some major professional bodies, especially where developments at NVQ Levels 4 and 5 are concerned. Instead, consortia of providers, such as business schools, are establishing their own verification arrangements to accommodate what they regard as the essentials of the professional preparation curriculum, within an NVQ framework. Certainly, the contrast with vocational education practice in some other European countries suggests that the professional and managerial sections of the English and Welsh workforce could be under-educated, and it is worth noting that the parallel arrangements to the NCVQ in Scotland have been put into place much more rapidly and with much closer cooperation from their further education colleges. Building on a good basis of general education, the Scottish Vocational Education Council (SCOTVEC) has implemented a modular system of vocational qualifications which prescribe both knowledge content and competence to be attained, in a way which has generally retained the confidence of their further education system.

By contrast, the NCVQ's policy brought about a very tense relationship with

BTEC, a body it needed to come to terms with in order to achieve its own performance targets. After all, BTEC is responsible for the registration of some 225,000 new students a year and it needed to be brought inside the NCVQ framework. In due course, if very slowly, the means were found to accommodate some of the most serious difficulties between the two. For one thing, NCVQ had powerful support in government, and could not afford to be seen to be failing in meeting its objectives; indeed, unlike the other examining and validating bodies, which are all limited companies, it has remained under the control of the ED. Partly for that reason, it has been a significant factor in the continuing argument over post-16 education between the DFE and the ED. Eventually, in August 1993, the NCVQ issued its document, *The Common Accord*,[12] which sets out the assessment and verification procedures releating to all its NVQ awards. It defines the roles in quality assurance for both the awarding bodies and the organizations they approve to offer them. As we have seen, industry lead bodies had been gradually established to cover all the main employment sectors, and awarding body status for NVQs was granted to all the existing further education examining and validating bodies. By May 1995, there were 130 of these awarding bodies, which suggests that only a modest rationalization had been achieved of the situation which the NCVQ was intended to simplify. It had not significantly affected the traditional proliferation of award-giving and standard-setting organizations, and many vested interests had managed to survive its drive for simplicity in the training system. In practice, many existing qualifications were given conditional approval by the NCVQ before they had been converted to a competence-based system of accreditation, so the rapid and wholesale change to their curricula was much slower in coming than the colleges had feared. Indeed, some vocational teachers, helped by their professional associations, embraced the changes very readily. Among the most successful were the hairdressers, who rapidly switched to a competence-based approach, to which their practical courses lent themselves. There are some interesting examples of departments which used the NVQ structure to offer units of training to young people and to employed hairdressers, as well as those wanting to update their knowledge, all supported by an NCVQ-approved assessment system, sometimes with self-study materials to cover the necessary related knowledge. At the same time, larger commercial salons were able to take over the training and accreditation of their own staff, using their industry lead body arrangements. In time, it is possible that such independent training arrangements may have an impact on the further education colleges, but the government's target of 50 per cent of the workforce aiming at NVQs by 1996 is sufficiently ambitious to provide enough work for all training providers. A recent report from the FEFC suggests that colleges are incurring substantial extra costs from introducing and implementing NVQs and from their slow acceptance by employers.[13]

These curricular changes in further education, prompted by a change in the assessment policies in the sector, have had a significant effect on all types of vocational training. In agriculture and horticulture, and in art and design, for example, the effects may have been more sharply felt because much of the work takes place in small, specialist colleges. The agricultural colleges and departments have had 30 years' experience of national proficiency tests, independently assessed by farmers and growers and have their own testing and awarding body, the National Examinations Board for Agriculture, Horticulture and Allied Industries (NEBAHAI), the largest body of its kind in the field. They have also had considerable experience of financial autonomy, running farms, gardens and residential centres. They have recently broadened their curriculum, both to respond to increased diversity in the industry and also to ensure their future viability. Therefore, they do not fit neatly into a categorization of lead bodies catering solely for agriculture, which in any case have not met the needs of small farmers. More importantly, perhaps, many farmers have been unable to deal with the paperwork involved in workplace assessment and have wanted the college to handle all assessment tasks for them. Nevertheless, in the above-mentioned annual report for 1993–94, the FEFC inspectorate reported that the agricultural colleges were particularly highly regarded and that agricultural education is carried out by dedicated staff in well-equipped colleges. There is a danger, however, that as many of these colleges are rather small and expensive to run, it may prove difficult to sustain them.

In art education, foundation courses which have prepared students for specialist degree courses are in the process of being overtaken by developments in awards. Previously carrying no awards, they were brought into the scope of BTEC's Diploma in Foundation Studies in Art and Design. Because the National Council for Foundation Education in Art and Design has decided to withdraw certification from foundation and other access courses and because many of the art colleges are unhappy with the BTEC courses, a group of them, together with the southern RAC, have recently launched a new National Board for Foundation Studies in Art and Design. The new board will award its first national diplomas in the summer of 1995. Meanwhile, foundation courses now look very like GNVQs, which in other disciplines offer direct entry into higher education. A difficulty for specialist art and design courses is that the GNVQ has only been introduced as a general course, and specialist BTEC National Diplomas in such areas as photography and graphic design will find no place in its structure. Meanwhile, as commented on by the 1993–94 FEFC inspectorate report, art colleges have some difficulty in justifying the cost of one-to-one student teaching in their courses. While the demand for art and design courses remains high, the prospects of obtaining directly related employment are not good.

The problem of how to provide work-based training and qualifications for those who had opted for full-time education post-16 remains. In addition, there is the continuing tension between the academic and vocational traditions of post-16 education embedded in the history of our educational system. On the one side are school sixth forms and most sixth-form colleges, offering mainly A-level courses, with GCSE repeats and some vocational foundation courses for the less academically able. On the other are further education colleges, usually in the same neighbourhood, with predominantly vocational courses, often to first degree level, with A-level and GCSE courses for those who needed a second chance to obtain them. In the middle are those colleges designated or aspiring to be tertiary, with substantial full-time course provision for the majority of the 16 to 19 age group in their area, with large numbers of GCE A-level students covering a wide age range, and a comprehensive range of full-time and part-time vocational courses. Many of these colleges had regretfully acknowledged the narrowness of the experience of A-level students by importing additional elements into their curriculum, sometimes as a result of participation in TVEI, and by giving their students the opportunity to benefit from the college's vocational resources. Information technology training, electronics A/S-level courses for physics students, supplementary modern languages for business students, and aspects of art and design are typical examples.

At the same time, the government had firmly rejected all attempts to broaden the GCE A-level curriculum. For example, it turned down the recommendation of the 1988 Higginson Committee[14] that A-levels should be broadened to comprise five subjects, while the School Examinations and Assessment Council (SEAC) conducted extensive consultations about the principles upon which A-levels should be based, and then in 1993 tightened up the criteria by which it was prepared to permit A-levels to be based on modular programmes which allowed some element of flexibility and student choice. It had eventually to be accepted, albeit reluctantly by many educationists and others, that the main features of A-level courses would remain unchanged. Meanwhile, there were suggestions from the government itself about ways in which the academic–vocational divide might be bridged, and new diplomas were proposed, awarded on the basis of obtaining A-level or GCSE passes in combination with BTEC units or NVQs. Kenneth Baker, when Secretary of State for Education, suggested in 1990 that the divide might be bridged by introducing the teaching of core skills into all full-time courses as a unifying force. The search was on for 'parity of esteem' between academic and vocational qualifications, though how this could be achieved when the government publicly proclaimed that A-level must be maintained as 'the gold standard' was not at all clear.

Against this background, the idea that all BTEC and other integrated courses should be converted to an NVQ-type competence base, assessed in the workplace, was becoming increasingly unacceptable to course managers who were having to cater for rapidly increasing numbers of full-time students. For many students who wanted a full-time education post-16 with a vocational slant, the BTEC National Diploma represented a genuine and attractive alternative to A-levels, as it both provided a broad general education and also could offer entrance to higher education. The other further education examining bodies offered similar courses which they were equally reluctant to convert to a purely competence base. As a result, the NCVQ was persuaded by the DFE to offer a GNVQ designed for full-time students, on the basis of competence assessment with performance criteria, but with a substantial element of general education contained in a specification for the core skills of communication, application of number, information technology, personal skills and problem-solving, and, eventually, a modern foreign language.[15] Assessment would be in the hands of teaching staff, although evidence could be gathered from work experience as well as classroom performance. In 1992–93, its first year of development, the GNVQ was offered at Level 2, for those with very modest GCSE success, and Level 3 for those with four or more good GCSE passes, a common entrance requirement for A-level study. BTEC, C&G and the RSA all contributed to its development, with the NCVQ holding overall responsibility. The qualification was initially offered in only five vocational areas, but was rapidly expanded to others, and is intended to cover all areas relevant to full-time further education students by 1996–97. Despite the comprehensive assessment arrangements implied by competence assessment, the DFE insisted that formal written tests should also be included in the assessment of the compulsory units of the courses. While this was an attempt to inject into the programmes some of the 'rigour' of A-levels, it was also designed to ensure some measure of comparability between the variants offered by the different examining bodies. However, since these bodies designed, set and marked their own examinations, initially this met only with limited success. The NCVQ was therefore poised to exercise some degree of coordinating influence over the standards of further education examining bodies similar to that which the new Schools Curriculum and Assessment Authority (SCAA) could exercise over the GCE boards. The first courses at Level 1 were introduced in the second year of the GNVQs' operation, although BTEC declined to offer them. These comprise mandatory and optional units, while there is the possibility of adding units, which might be standard NVQs or A-level courses. Thus, GNVQs appear to offer an opportunity to combine academic and vocational study into a single qualification and, though still in their early stages, have been enthusiastically welcomed by many students, both in the further education sector and also in schools. Indeed, the early 1995 returns from the three awarding bodies (BTEC, C&G and the RSA), indicate that about one in four of young people coming through the education system are already taking GNVQs. Further, the Dearing review of the National Curriculum for Schools has proposed that 14- to 16-year-olds should be able to include a partial GNVQ award as part of their regular studies, and BTEC has declared its intention of withdrawing its National Diploma as soon as sufficient variants of GNVQ have been developed. Thus, the impact of the various policies of the two government departments concerned, the DFE and the ED, on the reform of post-16 education and training has been very substantial and is well documented in a recent book on the subject from the Centre for Education and Industry at Warwick University.[16]

The major attraction of GNVQs for many young people has been the posibility of an alternative route into higher education which is vocational, or combines vocational and academic study. To help nourish GNVQs, a committee of the Universities' Central Admissions Scheme has worked steadily to improve awareness of them among higher education admissions tutors. The summer of 1994 has shown that many of the first group of students with GNVQs achieved their goal of entry to higher education, a situation which is being very carefully monitored. It is clear that while these students are not generally among the most able academically and might have been reluctant to embark on an experimental programme, many of them have nevertheless demonstrated an impressive level of achievement in some of the personal qualities which make for success in higher education, such as organizing themselves well and effectively evaluating their progress. Performance at these characteristics contributes to the grading of the GNVQ students' achievement, a factor which further complicates the selection process for admissions tutors used simply to basing their decisions largely on the scores from A-level grades. Consequently some universities have set up 'compacts' or partnerships with local providers of GNVQs, in order to improve the familiarity of their staff with the very different demands which GNVQs make on students as compared with A-levels. These compacts guarantee applicants an interview, so that they have the opportunity to explain the work they have done. The progression of the students through the system, and the correlation between their success and their entry grades and study patterns, is being monitored through a series of research projects run by the awarding bodies, and by a study funded by the Nuffield Foundation and the FEU.[17] What may eventually emerge is a study route which is respectable and valued in its own right. However, as the government has consistently supported A-levels as the 'gold standard', GNVQs have to earn a similar level of respect if they are to achieve parity of esteem.[18] Indeed, in the short time for which they have been operating, GNVQs have attracted concern about weaknesses in course design and slackness in assessing students' work. While these criticisms, made trenchantly in a report issued by the Office for Standards in Education (OFSTED) in the autumn of 1994, apply specifically to schools offering

GNVQs, the FEFC inspectorate has reported teething problems in further education colleges, including poor advice to students before starting, high drop-out rates and 'variable' assessment. The last point is underlined by an ED-sponsored report by the University of London Institute of Education, which came out at about the same time as the OFSTED report: it indicated that grading standards in centres were not consistent and that the system of assessment currently in use would not be able to establish comparable standards betwen centres in the near future. Clearly, GNVQs have some way to go before they earn a similar level of respect to that of A-levels.

Some of the issues involved in the post-16 curriculum debate are identified by Noel Kershaw,[19] who makes a plea for some common ground in the curriculum, through the achievement of similar educational aims even if they are through different routes. By developing core skills in either A-levels or vocational courses, and by recognizing achievement in programmes which combine elements of the vocational and the academic, it is possible to establish a system which will encourage further study rather than declare failure, and render the concept of 'equivalence' unnecessary. Many colleges are struggling with the idea of modularizing their curriculum in order to provide flexibility in what they offer to their students, but they are handicapped by the absence of a recognized system for giving credit to flexible study. Some examples are to be found locally, for instance through some 'open college' agreements, whereby students can carry 'passports' from one period of study to another. Nationally, however, there is no such arrangement, except within the NROVA. However, this has not yet become fully established as a way of negotiating entry to higher education, for instance, although some employers are prepared to look at this kind of portfolio during recruitment. Another possible initiative along these lines is to be found in the White Paper *Competitiveness: Helping Business to Win*, published in May 1994.[20] It puts forward various proposals, if not many new ones, for improving skill levels in industry for the economic good of the country, including one for a new general diploma for 16-year-olds, to set a baseline of achievement which would recognize both academic and vocational studies. A similar proposal for 18-year-olds, which recommended combining both kinds of study as a preparation for both employment and higher education, was included in the Conservative Party manifesto at the 1992 election, but appears to have come to nothing.

So far, this chapter has concentrated on the impact of the examining and validating bodies, together with the NCVQ, on the further education curriculum. There are, of course, other players in the game. One of the most prominent was, as we have seen, the FEU, established by government in 1977 to provide advice and information to the further education sector and to fund research and development. Its initial brief was to oversee the development of courses for young people, especially the UVP scheme, which was to be run jointly by the DFE and the ED. Its remit now includes the review of curricula offered by further education institutions, the development of further education by carrying out specific studies, the dissemination of information on the process of curriculum development, and the promotion of quality in further education provision. Since its establishment, it has established regional offices, mainly alongside the RACs, and expanded its staff and publications work. Its support to the colleges faced with a rapidly changing system has been important. Thus, through development projects it has funded work in colleges to enable change to be effected, monitored and written up for the benefit of others, including such important areas as vocational preparation, flexible course delivery systems, and adult guidance. It has also supported national initiatives such as YTS, TVEI, and GNVQs, by offering advice on ways of implementing change both to government departments and to colleges. Its many publications comprise one of the few sources of research and advice available to the further education sector, where relatively little academic research work is done by other agencies.

To a lesser extent, and in different ways, the Further Education Staff College (FESC) has also had an effect on the further education curriculum. While its remit has been different from that of the FEU, being primarily concerned with improving the efficiency of the sector through the training of senior college managers, it has also conducted research in the sector, and has been able to run projects for other agencies, including the ED. Inevitably, there has been work which had an interest in, and an impact on, the further education curriculum, for example its 'Responsive College' project, which sought to examine and improve the relationship of colleges to their markets. Increased emphasis was given to the need for colleges to be more flexible in the way they offered their wares to potential students, with implications for delivery and the design of courses.

Both these bodies have supported college staff as they moved into the 'new age' of further education, where the student is increasingly regarded as an individual, is given guidance in the choice of programmes of study, especially those which take account of, and sometimes give credit for, existing experience; where teaching may be designed to meet individual needs, and may not require consistent college attendance; where learning is supported by a variety of resources, including information technology; and where accreditation for this learning is given through some of the new systems described above. The fact that colleges still have some way to go in these subjects is recognized by the funding councils which, as we have seen, have reviewed the roles of the FEU and the FESC and have concluded that their contributions to the further education sector are sufficiently useful and distinctive for them to carry on their work, in combination, under the auspices of a new Further Education Development Agency

(FEDA). Among the responsibilities of this new body, being established in April 1995, is to 'assist the students' needs, and thereby to contribute to the achievement of the national education and training targets'.[21]

As has been clear from the foregoing account, the relationship between the ED and the further education sector in recent years has been an uncomfortable, but productive, one. Despite the difficulties of the relationship, the ED has, through its funding of a variety of schemes, effected considerable change in the colleges, probably to a greater extent than the DFE. This was achieved by offering the colleges funds, which they needed to survive, but always with conditions attached to them. The results have included college programmes for young people with poor employment prospects, for adult unemployed people, for women returning to work after bringing up their families, and for people changing careers in mid-life. Other ED-sponsored initiatives to which the colleges have responded are the TVEI programme, the establishment of the NCVQ, and programmes of many kinds which support small businesses, self-employed people, and the unemployed. Some of these initiatives have also benefited from European Community (EC) funds and, as a consequence, have played an important part in helping to deliver EC policy directives, translated into schemes which supported economic development through training. At the higher levels of course provision, colleges have created significant overlaps with the work of at least the new universities, in the move to expand rapidly the opportunities for higher education study. Most colleges have had higher-level courses on offer in their major curriculum areas for many years, carefully guarded by principals and teaching staff as indications of the colleges' expertise. Advanced technicians courses, such as the Higher National Diploma, provided a basis for degree-level work in a few colleges. This work has been subject to the vagaries of the funding mechanisms over the last few years, and colleges have had to move rapidly to secure funding council permission to run these courses.

As a consequence, further education has become an important route into higher education, and in some colleges a student can pursue a course of study from GCSE to postgraduate level. For those whose educational careers have been interrupted there are other routes into higher education and, as we have seen, many colleges now offer access courses, which provide a way for well-motivated adults to get into university without following the conventional A-level route. In all these ways, the curricula offered by the average college are today dramatically different from those of 15 years ago, both in content and style of delivery. Similarly, the student population of colleges has changed and draws upon a broader base of population than in the past. While the three main variants of the further education curriculum described at the beginning of this chapter remain, the increased focus on the learning needs of individual students has led to much greater ingenuity in the ways in which the various elements are combined to suit particular learners. The result is increased expertise in curriculum design on the part of teachers, and less reliance on the prescriptions of the various agencies who have controlled the further education curriculum in the past. That this should be the case at a time when the government is increasing its prescriptions over the standards of what should be taught, and how they should be assessed, is likely to offer some interesting challenges to the continuing ingenuity of further education managers in the colleges.

Notes and References

1   National Curriculum Council, *Core Skills 16–19*, London, NCC, a response to the Secretary of State, 1990.
2   B. Pratley, *Signposts*, London, Further Education Unit, 1980.
3   Manpower Services Commission, *A New Training Initiative: An Agenda for Action*, Consultative Document, Sheffield, MSC, 1981; and Employment Department, White Paper, *A New Training Initiative: A Programme for Action*, Cmnd 8455, London, HMSO, 1981.
4   Institute of Manpower Studies, *Foundation Training Issues*, Sheffield, Manpower Services Commission, 1982; and Further Education Staff College, *Work-based Learning Terms*, London, Training Agency/HMSO, 1989.
5   Employment Department/Department of Education and Science, White Paper, *Working Together – Education and Training*, Cmnd 9823, London, HMSO, 1986.
6   L. M. Cantor and I. F. Roberts, *Further Education Today: A Critical Review*, London, Routledge & Kegan Paul, 1986 (3rd edn), pp. 44–45.
7   Further Education Unit, *From Coping to Confidence: A Staff Development Resource Pack for FE Teachers*, London, DES/FEU, 1985. This was the first of a series of publications from FEU designed to assist teachers to respond to this new group of students.
8   Further Education Unit, *A Basis for Choice*, London, FEU, 1979.
9   Employment Department/Department of Education and Science, *White Paper, Working Together – Education and Training, op. cit.*
10 G. Jessup, *Outcomes: NVQs and the Emerging Model of Education and Training*, London, Falmer Press, 1981.
11 A. Smithers, *All our Futures*, Manchester, Manchester University Centre for Education and Employment Research, 1993. For a detailed analysis of the Smithers critique, see T. Hyland, 'Tilting at windmills: the problems of challenging the National Council for Vocational Qualifications', *Educational Studies*, **20**(2), pp. 251–265 (1994).
12 National Council for Vocational Training, *The Common Accord*, London, NCVQ, August 1993.
13 Further Education Funding Council for England, *National Vocational Qualifications in the Further Education Sector in England*, Report from the Inspectorate, Coventry, FEFC, September 1994.
14 DES, *Advancing A Levels (The Higginson Report)*, London, HMSO, 1988.
15 See ED/DES, White Paper, *Education and Training for the 21st Century*, Cmnd. 1536, London, HMSO, 1991, and subsequent requests from the Secretary of State for Education.

16 W. Richardson, J. Woodhouse and D. Finegold (eds.), *The Reform of Post-16 Education and Training in England and Wales*, London, Longman, 1993.

17 Major studies are in progress at the National Foundation for Educational Research and at the University of London Institute of Education. See, for example, A. Wolf, R. Burgess, H. Stott, and J. Veasey, *GNVQ Assessment Review Project*, London, University of London Institute of Education, May 1994; and FEU/London Institute of Education, *The Evolution of GNVQ*, London, Nuffield Foundation, November, 1994.

18 B. Pratley, 'Yes, Ministers', *Times Educational Supplement*, 4 March 1994, p. 21.

19 N. Kershaw, *An Unfinished Jigsaw: the 16+ Curriculum in the 1990s,* Glasgow, Further Education Staff College/Association for Colleges, 1994.

20 Employment Department/Department for Trade and Industry, *Competitiveness: Helping Business to Win*, White Paper, Cmnd 2563, London, HMSO, May 1994.

21 'A Development Agency for FE', *EDUCA*, **136**, 7 (1993).

Four

Students in Further Education

As we have seen, the further education sector in England and Wales presently caters for more than 2,800,000 students, who attend a bewildering array of programmes on a variety of bases of study. The vast majority of these students are over 16 years of age and they include a growing proportion of mature students – usually defined as having spent at least three years after the end of compulsory schooling away from study – who may be of any age from 19 to 90, and conceivably older. Colleges are also beginning to recruit youngsters in the 14 to 16 age range, so that altogether they cater for a greater variety of students than any other institutions in our education system. The complexities that arise have led one member of a college senior management team to describe the situation, aptly enough, in these terms: 'The classic further education college has hundreds of rooms and tens of thousands of students, doing everything from nursery nursing to things that can be half a day long. Managing that is a nightmare'.[1] Thus, the realities of life in a typical further education college are that students are constantly coming and going throughout the day and into the evening, attending courses on different bases of study.

In order to collect statistics of student numbers in colleges on which to base their funding mechanisms, the funding councils have devised what they call 'the most appropriate breakdown' of modes of attendance into no fewer than nine categories. These comprise: full-time attendance, by which they mean 30 weeks or more in a year; full-time, consisting of attendance for at least four but less than 30 weeks; 'sandwich' programmes, in which the students spend part of their course gaining practical experience in business or industry; block release, by which employers release their employees to attend college for a continuous period of, say, three or four weeks; part-time day release, by which employees are released typically for one day a week; part-time attendance, in which students are not released by employers but presumably come of their own volition and in their own time; evening only, a self-explanatory category; open or distance learning, a method by which students work mainly at home; and, lastly, short courses which students attend full-time for less than four weeks.[2] For various reasons, not least because of this range of categories and the fact that

74

students are constantly coming and going to and from the colleges, precise numbers in the sector as a whole are notoriously difficult to count accurately. As money from the funding councils to the colleges is closely related to student numbers, it is widely accepted that when making returns to the funding councils, some colleges indulge, understandably perhaps, in a degree of 'creative accounting'. In order to ensure that colleges do not exaggerate their student numbers, the Further Education Funding Council for England (FEFC) is currently devising a mechanism to prevent this happening.[3] However, a reasonably accurate picture of the numbers of further education students in England can be gained from FEFC statistics (Table 4.1). Two years after incorporation, in 1993–94, they totalled an estimated 674,000 in full-time and sandwich courses, and just over 2 million in various forms of part-time courses, including day and block release, evening only, and open or distance learning. Of the total of 2,700,000, 60 per cent were in general further education colleges, and although the FEFC has not included detailed statistics, it is likely that women students outnumber men. Over the years the numbers of students attending colleges in the various categories have changed relative to one another. In particular, in recent years, those on full-time and open and distance learning programmes have increased, while those attending on a part-time basis have progressively declined, for example by some 7 per cent in 1993, according to recent FEFC figures, though there were some indications at the end of 1994 that the numbers of students on employer-sponsored day-release courses were picking up again. The reasons for these shifts in student populations will be discussed later in this chapter.

Another way of categorizing further education students is according to the types of curriculum they are undertaking. Broadly speaking, these fall into four major groups: those which are primarily 'academic' or non-vocational in nature, including GCE A-level; those which are job specific and closely linked to the world of work; those which provide a general introduction to vocational areas; and those which are recreational. For example, in a pamphlet 'The New Qualifications Framework',[4] issued in March 1994, the Department for Education (DFE) outlines as a brief guide to young people aged 16 or over, three types of qualifications which they can study to prepare them for entry into higher education or work. These are, respectively,'general education' – GCSE, GCE A-levels and AS-levels; 'vocational education' – General National Vocational Qualifications (GNVQs); and 'training for jobs' – National Vocational Qualifications (NVQs). Traditionally, the staple diet of the further education colleges has consisted of their vocational training courses, which range over a large number of subject areas from agriculture and art and design through business studies, engineering, and hotel and catering and health and community studies, to mathematics and computer studies. The popularity

Table 4.1. All-Year Student Enrolments in Further Education Institutions in England, 1992–93, and Estimates for 1993–94 ('000)

A.	By mode of attendance	1992–93 (actual)	1993–94 estimated
	Full-time and sandwich	621	674
	Block and part-time released	459	
	Other part-time and evening only	1249	} 2027
	Open or distance learning	73	
	Short courses[a]		
	Totals	2391	2701
B.	**By types of colleges**		
	General further education colleges	1640	1657
	Tertiary colleges	431	425
	Sixth-form colleges	100	112
	Colleges of agriculture and horticulture	34	35
	Colleges of art and design	10	10
	Designated institutions[b]	177	462
	Totals	2392	2701

[a]Fewer than 500 enrolments. [b]Including adult education colleges and Workers' Educational Association.
Source: *FEFC Statistics Bulletin,* Issue Number 3, February 1995.

of these subject areas varies from time to time in relation to a number of factors, including the sex of the students and job opportunities. For example, one can get some idea of the profile of vocational education and training in the country by comparing the examination entries of the major awarding bodies. While these statistics are not to be taken literally because of the different structure of awards and the ways in which the figures are compiled, they do give a general idea of the relative popularity of the major areas of vocational education.[5] For example, an analysis of the City and Guilds (C&G) statistics for 1992–93 shows that the most popular areas of study were commerce and training with 24 per cent of the total 'unit entries', general education and work preparation with 17.5 per cent, vehicle and plant maintenance with 12.2 per cent, electrical and electronic engineering with 10 per cent, beauty and care with 9.3 per cent and construction with 5.7 per cent.[6] Figures for Business and Technology Education Council (BTEC) 'new registrations' for the previous year reveal a broadly similar picture, with the largest number of students registering for programmes in business and finance, followed by engineering, science and catering, and construction. One point of interest that emerges from these figures is that many students still undertake programmes in engineering or construction despite predictions of the virtual collapse of these industries.[7]

However, in our view a more revealing way of classifying further education students is by means of broad groups derived from personal characteristics which transcend the categories described above. Accordingly, we shall use five such major groupings: students in the age range of 16 to 18 or 19; adult learners; students for whom special provisions are made; students aged 14 to 16; and those undertaking courses of higher education.

Students aged 16 to 19

This age group has always featured very largely in the further education sector and since the sixth-form colleges became part of the sector in April 1993, their relative importance has increased. This follows inevitably, since the sixth-form colleges, which cater almost exclusively for this age group, now make up approximately one-fifth of the institutions in the further education sector. Moreover, as we have seen, for the last few years, more and more 16-year-olds are staying on in full-time education and training after the ending of compulsory schooling.

Consequently, it is not surprising that well over half of all the students undertaking GCE A-level courses, the great majority of whom are aged between 16 and 19, are doing so in colleges in the further education sector. However, as we have already pointed out, by their very nature sixth-form colleges differ in their student populations from general further education colleges. The former are likely to remain relatively small institutions, largely offering full-time day 'academic' programmes of one or two years' duration leading to the award of GCSEs, GCE A-levels and GNVQs. They are beginning to diversify a little, being free to extend the range of their courses into vocational areas and to recruit adult students. However, for some years to come these other activities are likely to be only a small part of the work of sixth-form colleges, whereas, of course, they feature very largely in the provision made by general further education colleges.

One matter of considerable concern for all the colleges who cater for this age group is that far too high a proportion of their students fail to complete their programmes of study or to achieve qualifications at the end of it. This problem was highlighted in the study undertaken jointly by the Audit Commission and the Office for Standards in Education (OFSTED), published in 1993 under the title, *Unfinished Business: Full-Time Educational Courses for 16–19 Year Olds.*[8] While acknowledging that accurate completion rates were difficult to assess because not all institutions recorded the information, the report estimated that nationally every year about 150,000 students who enrol on 16 to 19 courses either fail their examinations or leave their courses early. In the 42 schools and colleges studied, an average of 13 per cent of students failed to complete GCE A-levels, while some 18 per cent dropped out of vocational courses. In some schools and colleges, the non-completion rate was as high as 80 per cent, an appalling state of affairs. The cost to the colleges of this wastage is estimated to be of the order of £330 million pounds a year, while the cost to the students in wasted time and loss of self-esteem is incalculable. There may, of course, be extenuating circumstances: for example, a student may leave a vocational course part way through in order to accept a job offer. Nevertheless, it is incontestable that far too many students taken on courses by colleges, presumably considered capable of successfully completing them and passing the examinations, fail to do so. As the Further Education Unit (FEU) has pointed out in a number of studies of the problem of student drop-out,[9] it is a complex process which, while having much to do with the prior expectations, personal characteristics and circumstances of the students, also includes many course and institutional factors which are within the colleges' control. A BTEC report on the subject[10] arrives at similar conclusions, affirming that what it calls 'personal attention' is the basic principle behind good retention rates, and that, in order to tackle the problem of drop-out, it needs to be clearly defined and understood. An important contributory factor to high drop-out rates is the lack of basic literacy and numeracy skills on the part of many students. According to a survey published by the Adult Literacy and Basic Skills Unit (ALBSU) early in 1993, about 40 per cent of students surveyed, most of whom were aged 16 to 19 and studying for GCE A-levels, GCSEs and vocational qualifications, were unable to cope with relatively simple literacy and numeracy tests and had skills below the levels expected of 14-year-olds. Perhaps the conclusion to be drawn is that the further education colleges should provide remedial programmes to help improve this unhappy state of affairs. Meanwhile, both the Audit Commission in their report and the FEU in their studies make a number of recommendations designed to minimize student drop-out from courses and to maximize the number who pass their examinations. Among the Audit Commission's recommendations are that schools and colleges should record full and accurate pre-course data about students and track the rates of successful completion, unsuccessful completion and non-completion for all courses and, unsurprisingly, that they should 'take action to remedy unsuccesful course outcomes and to reduce excess costs';[11] and that the funding councils should establish funding structures which retain open access to post-16 education as a whole but do not encourage indiscriminate student recruitment to courses. The FEU's advice directed to the colleges is that they should provide more pre-course contact with students, establish a well-structured form of induction to the college for students, and ensure that their classroom experience is appropriate and well-organized, that appropriate advice and guidance are made available and that a welcoming college environment is provided.

While all these are desirable objectives, the fact remains that colleges and their staff are under considerable pressure to recruit students and, in many cases, their conditions of employment leave them little time to provide students with the detailed, personal help which they need if they are to do well on their courses. Nevertheless, the high wastage rates which have so long afflicted the further education sector are, or should be, unacceptable and any sensible measures which result in their diminution are to be welcomed. It is, however, difficult to believe that the situation will greatly improve in coming years.

One way of improving retention rates is by devising a range of appropriate curricula for the 16 to 19 age group. As we have seen, one of the most important curricular developments in recent years is the introduction of GNVQs, whose features were described and analysed in the last chapter. To judge by its uptake, this seems to have met a pressing need: in 1993–94, for example, there were some 70,000 entrants and in 1994–95 this number more that doubled to 165,000, the great majority of them in the 16 to 19 age group. However, the introduction of a new qualification alone is no guarantee of standards, and it is significant that the National Council for Vocational Qualifications (NCVQ) has warned that it will be difficult to improve and monitor quality without extra resources, needed to train assessors and possibly to establish its own inspectorate.[12]

Most of the students taking these courses do so on a full-time basis; for example, the numbers of full-time students funded by the FEFC increased by 8 per cent between 1992–93 and 1993–94, from 570,000 to 617,000. By contrast, part-time student numbers scarcely increased at all over the same period, from 1,509,000 to 1,518,000. Indeed, in one major category, namely trainees released by employers for part-time study on a day-release or block-release basis, student numbers actually declined, by 7 per cent. There are a number of contributory factors to this decline. Firstly, with the UK only very slowly pulling out of recession and with unemployment still high, many employers are reluctant to recruit workers who require training: in the building industry, for example, the numbers of young people brought in through the youth training programme have halved in the last two years. Secondly, the release of young employees to attend part-time college courses was, and remains, very patchy, with considerable differences between individual industries and between young men and young women. Thirdly, the recent cuts in discretionary awards by local education authorities (LEAs), which we discussed in an earlier chapter, has resulted in some students being unable to take college courses. Finally, the application of the '21-hour rule', whereby an individual may qualify for unemployment benefit and income support provided he or she does not attend college for more than 21 hours and has to leave the college course if offered a job, has inevitably resulted in some drop-out and failure to obtain qualifications, as have the recent changes whereby unemployment benefits can be withdrawn after six months from those who have not found employment in that time. As from April 1995, the number of hours an unemployed student on benefit can study are being changed from 21 hours of supervised study to 16 guided learning hours. Whether this will make it easier or more difficult for students on benefit to continue with their education remains to be seen. The failure of part-time student numbers to increase significantly makes it unlikely that many colleges will meet their national targets of increasing their populations by 8 per cent for 1994–95, something which is a matter of considerable concern both to the funding councils and to the Training and Enterprise Councils (TECs). In order to improve the situation, the former are devising a funding formula to encourage the sustained expansion of part-time courses, and many of the latter are offering colleges cash bonuses to achieve local targets for education and training programmes.

Adult Learners

Just how many 'adult learners' there are in the UK depends upon the definition that is used. Clearly, if it included all those adults – over the age of 18 or 21, as the case may be – who were involved in one form of learning or another, then the number would be enormous, and many of them would have been involved in continuous study since they entered school at the age of 5. However, the term is normally used to define those who, having completed their full-time education, then re-enter some form of post-school eduction after some years' absence. By this definition, there are some 6 million adult learners: 3.4 million are in what is generally called 'the formal sector', and 1.6 million are in adult education centres, 800,000 in further education, and the rest in university extra-mural departments, higher education institutions, including the Open University, and adult residential colleges.[13] The remaining 2.6 million who fall outside the formal sector are either provided for by a range of bodies, including employers, trades unions, voluntary bodies, distance-learning bodies and the media, or provide for themselves by independent learning, in local libraries for example. We are here mainly concerned with the 800,000 adult learners studying, very largely part-time, in further education institutions. Among them, the number who wish to obtain vocational qualifications in further education has increased in recent years, as have those undertaking access courses which, when successfully completed, enable them to enter a programme of higher education. In addition, there is an increasing number of inter-institutional arrangements, such as the Open College Networks (OCNS) scheme and consortia of colleges offering access programmes, which have come into existence to promote adult learning. The upshot is that distinctions between what is offered in adult education centres and further education colleges are becoming less marked, while at the same time the scale and variety of adult learning has grown considerably.

However, traditionally, provision for adult learning has been divided into four broad categories. The first consists of courses which are work-related, and many of which lead to vocational qualifications; they also include courses of occupational preparation for the unemployed, for women returning to work and for those seeking marketing skills. The second category comprises courses which include access and other 'second chance' provision and those termed 'role preparation', such as preparing people for retirement, courses for school and college governors, and trade union studies. The third is basic or special adult learning such as programmes in adult literacy and numeracy, and provision for those with special educational needs. Finally, there is general education, including non-vocational provision in such areas as the humanities, art and craft, modern languages, the performing arts, science and music. So complex and varied is all this provision that an HMI report on the subject comments fairly, if rather tartly, 'nationally, the co-ordination of adult education is hindered by its diversity and its planning by the lack of an agreed definition and mutually compatible statistics'.[14] This diversity of provision is reflected in the large range of programmes, many of them part-time, available to adults in a general further education college. However, as a recent FEU report points out, in its own form of shorthand, 'At a time when adult enrolments are overtaking those of young people, college cultures still assume a 17-year-old norm.'[15]

Since the passing of the 1992 Further and Higher Education Act, courses funded by the funding councils under Schedule 2 of the Act, with a few specified exceptions, have to be strictly vocational with recognized qualifications at the end of them. These are defined as courses preparing students for vocational qualifications, GCSE and GCE A- and AS-levels, access courses, basic English or mathematics, English as a second language, literacy in Welsh, and 'independent living and communication skills' for people with learning difficulties which prepare them for the above courses. All other adult education has to depend on local authority support and fees. However, as we have seen in the previous chapter, this draconian legislation failed to take into account the fact that many adult learners use courses which are non-vocational for their own vocational purposes.[16] As things stand, if local authority adult education centres wish to offer courses which are eligible for support from the funding councils, they will only get funds if they can persuade a further education college to bid for the money and then subcontract the work to them. How widespread this practice now is it is difficult to say; however, last year, for example, Kent County Council received approximately 8 per cent of its annual adult education budget from the FEFC to provide specific courses, but the county may be atypical. Certainly, what has been dubbed 'the contract culture' has come in for considerable criticism on the grounds that it has reduced the resources available for adult education. At the time of the passing of the 1992 Act, there was very considerable concern that traditional adult education would be gravely damaged by the new funding arrangements. Happily, this does not seem to have happened and there has only been a marginal drop in participation rates in the last few years.[17] This is probably largely due to increasing demand from students, and masks the fact that many local authorities are finding it increasingly difficult to fund adult education and that many adults are forced to drop out of courses because of financial difficulties.

As far as the courses are concerned, many providers are moving towards accrediting more of them for adults. This is partly in order to gain funding under Schedule 2 of the 1992 Act, and partly because more students are anxious to obtain qualifications either in response to the requirements of employers or because they desire access to higher education. Colleges are also seeking to modularize some of their courses so that parts of them can be accredited. For this purpose, many of them are turning to OCNs, which were created to open access routes for learners from non-professional backgrounds by providing vocational training through open and flexible learning. Emanating from the Open College established in Manchester, OCNs provide accreditation for learning outside national qualifications, offer quality assurance for learning programmes, many of which are recognized for access to higher education, and issue students with credits. Although access to this service is by no means without its problems, the National Open College Network (NOCN), which ensures that standards are consistent throughout the country, aims to have an OCN in operation or under development throughout England and Wales by the end of 1995.[18] Two recent marks of official approval are that the FEFC has approved OCN-accredited programmes as evidence of achievement for progression and as basic education under Schedule 2 of the 1992 Act, and the Employment Department (ED) has come to an agreement with the Open College that their credits can now count towards foundation and lifetime targets. OCNs have been particularly successful in designing and accrediting short courses which count towards a nationally recognized qualification, and in 1993–94 over 350,000 OCN credits were awarded to students. According to a recent FEU survey,[19] some 900 organizations are members of OCNs, including 370 institutions of further and higher education. OCNs seem to have attracted a higher proportion of non-traditional students than mainstream college courses, including those from ethnic minorities, the unwaged, women, and those with relatively low educational qualifications. These students often undertake learning programmes in order to progress to further study, and the opportunity to gain credit from them is valued as it raises self-esteem and motivates adult learners to further progress. However, such opportunities vary considerably across the country so that while the whole of Wales is covered by OCNs, in some parts of England they are at an early stage of development. Moreover, local authorities and individual TECs apply very different eligibility criteria to adults who apply for discretionary awards in order to undertake OCN-accredited courses. Nevertheless, the scale of the OCN enterprise is considerable: there are currently some 200 courses provided, mainly in vocational areas such as management, accountancy, education, nursing and caring. They also offer credits on NVQ courses from Levels 1 to 4 inclusive.

Whereas OCNs are a means of providing general access to learning, access programmes are specifically concerned with helping non-traditional students, without normal entry qualifications such as GCE A-levels, to enter higher education. These courses have grown rapidly in recent years and in 1993 there were nearly 900 of them, the vast majority of them offered by further education colleges, enrolling some 30,000 students, most of them women. The courses that are validated by access validating agencies, which are often regional consortia of universities and further education colleges, are very largely studied on a one-year full-time day, or two-year part-time basis, though some operate in the evenings. For the most part, they do not lead to any particular degree programme, though some, when satisfactorily completed, do guarantee entry to specific courses of higher education. Initially, students on access courses who passed them were awarded certificates of 'satisfactory completion'; recently, however, some of them have been awarded with grades in response to demands from university admission tutors. There is also evidence that some further education colleges are abandoning their access courses in favour of franchised degree courses with a foundation year.[20] As students on access courses do not receive a mandatory award from their local authorities, they are frequently dependent on discretionary grants which, as we have seen, have been reduced in number in recent years. Foundation years, when incorporated as part of a four-year degree programme and preparing a student in the same way as an access course, do carry the right to a mandatory award and assured progression on to a degree course. It is scarcely surprising, therefore, that the latter are growing at the expense of the former, especially in engineering, science, mathematics, computing, information technology and business and management, for which FEFC funding is markedly more generous than it is for arts subjects.

Three other areas of provision for adult learning, in which further education institutions are much involved, are programmes run in conjunction with the ALBSU, and with the Colleges of the Third Age (C3A), and those for the unemployed seeking help to prepare themselves to obtain employment. ALBSU defines basic skills as the ability to read, write and speak English and to use mathematics at a level necessary to function and progress at work and in society in general. Sadly, there are millions of adults in the UK who are deficient in one or more of these basic skills, and in order to help them many colleges, especially those located in metropolitan areas, have well-established centres which offer relevant programmes. Two recent developments in this field are the English for Speakers of Other Languages (ESOL) programmes and the family literacy initiative. The ESOL programmes attract a high proportion of adults of Asian origin and there is a growing demand from those who have entered the country as refugees from Eastern Europe and elsewhere. The aim of the family literacy initiative, sponsored by ALBSU with the help of a grant from the DFE, is to work with families in order to raise the basic skills of both children and adults. The C3A initiative, which began in the USA and first arrived in the United Kingdom in 1982, seeks to meet the needs of those who, having finished work, seek an active retirement. Clearly, the needs of individuals vary greatly; however, the C3A programmes try to provide a curriculum which enables them to have access to a wide range of educational activities. These may vary from place to place, often consisting of what is traditionally termed 'liberal adult education', while elsewhere providing courses in the handling of computers and their software, making use of facilities provided by further education colleges.[21]

Over the years, further education colleges have been much involved with providing programmes for unemployed adults – indeed, in some colleges they have comprised over 40 per cent of total enrolments.[22] Among the government-sponsored schemes introduced over the last decade or so are REPLAN, a programme of educational opportunities for unemployed adults which ended in 1991, PICKUP (Professional, Commercial and Industrial Updating), designed to help those in need of mid-career development, and RESTART, established in 1987, which is designed to inform unemployed people of jobs and other opportunities which might be available to them and to encourage them to seek jobs. However, the majority of unemployed adults in the colleges are taking part in 'mainstream' courses, always provided that they are 19 years of age or over, are studying for less than 21 hours a week – otherwise they lose benefits – and remain available for work. This '21-hour rule', which does not apply to students on special government schemes, has understandably attracted a great deal of criticism both from within and without further education. In order to damp down this criticism while retaining the 21-hour rule, the government introduced a new programme for unemployed adults in 1993, entitled Learning For Work, which aimed to return 30,000 of them to full-time education or training without loss of benefits. Initially, the scheme was welcomed by the colleges as providing some help for the unemployed at a time when discretionary grants were becoming less available.[23] However, it ran into financial problems quite soon, as the FEFC proved unwilling to provide extra money to support trainees on Learning For Work programmes. Consequently, it is unclear how many have actually enrolled on training courses. In any case, even if the full complement of trainees is recruited, it will represent only a drop in the ocean of those out of work, and many in the colleges and elsewhere consider it should be extended to all the long-term unemployed. Of that, however, there is virtually no prospect.

It is clear from the foregoing account that educational provision for adults in the further education sector is of major and growing importance. While, for the most part, the colleges have responded well to this development, and while student satisfaction with courses is high, adult education providers need to offer more flexible services, both in degree and delivery, to meet the needs of adults.[24] Among other things, they have been abjured to establish clear aims and objectives, collaborate to provide a balanced pattern of provision in a given area, develop systems which recognize an adult's prior learning and experience, provide more effective guidance, and respond flexibly to the diversity of needs of the great numbers of adult learners.[25] While the colleges would agree that all these are highly desirable objectives, attaining them at a time of great pressure and limited resources is very difficult, if not impossible.

Students with Special Requirements

The further education sector has long had an enviable reputation for the efforts it makes to cater for all sorts and conditions of students. Among the particular groups for whom it has increasingly made special provision in recent years are students from ethnic minorities, certain groups of women and students with special needs. The educational needs of students from ethnic minorities, while they have much in common with all other students, are in many ways different. By and large, they experience more difficulty in obtaining jobs than their contemporaries, for some of them English language skills may be at a premium, and they have their own cultural backgrounds and aspirations. In 1992, the FEU issued a bulletin and published an account of its work in 'ethnic monitoring' of further education college provision. Although it could be seen as a potentially controversial issue, it is regarded as important for its potential benefits, including the collection and analysis of information to assist future developments in such areas as making appropriate course provision, developing suitable marketing and complying with anti-discrimination legislation.[26] Among the findings that emerged from this admittedly limited study were that black students tended to be older than white students, enrol on low-level courses and be less well represented on employer-sponsored courses, while Asian women were under-represented in the college student population. To their credit, many colleges, especially those in the metropolitan areas where the ethnic minority communities are concentrated, have made increasingly successful efforts to cater for their needs. Special programmes include those for teaching students who do not have English as their first language to speak, read and write it, though these have not been helped by recent government cuts in the so-called 'Section 11' funding which is made available for this specific purpose, courses in Asian languages and access courses to facilitate entry into higher education. Colleges are also making particular efforts to recruit students from categories of the ethnic minorities, such as Asian adults and Afro-Caribbean men, who are under-represented. Inevitably, perhaps, given the difficult financial circumstances, the development of such provision has been piecemeal and rather slow in some areas. What are needed are more courses of the kind described above and further changes in curriculum and methodology tailored to the background and educational needs of students from the ethnic minorities.

Over recent years, in the further education sector in the United Kingdom, women students have progressively outnumbered men students. The same necessarily applies to England, as a recent DFE publication reveals.[27] Thus of the total of 1,407,000 adults aged 18 or over participating in further education in England that year, 828,000 were women and 579,000 were men. Interestingly enough, the numbers taking full-time courses were little different, with 103,000 women and 92,000 men, whereas in part-time courses women, numbering 725,000, greatly exceeeded the 487,000 men. Until fairly recently, men and women in the further education colleges studied very different programmes, with women predominating in the secretarial and caring subject areas and men in the engineering and technical fields, for example. While this is still largely the case, increasing numbers of women students are to be found undertaking programmes in the whole range of subject areas, including engineering and technology. A number of factors have contributed to this development, the most important of which perhaps has been the work of the Equal Opportunities Commission (EOC). The Technical and Vocational Education Initiative (TVEI) schemes introduced into schools have also helped. With their built-in equal-opportunities policies, they have stimulated the interest of girls in technological subjects, so that some of them have followed them by more advanced courses in these subjects in further education. Further education colleges have also targeted courses specifically at women, especially for those who wish to return to work. For example, an East Midlands college offers a 'Women in Information Technology' course for those who have been unemployed or unwaged for at least a year and who wish to obtain high-level qualifications in information technology; supported by the European Social Fund, the course offers free training for women seeking knowledge of computer-based systems and in supervisory management.

Another interesting offering is the access course at the City of Liverpool Community College for women who wish to obtain high-level qualifications in architecture, building and related fields. These kinds of courses are frequently designed to meet the needs of women with families and are timetabled as flexibly as possible and provide crèche and playgroup facilities. These developments have also taken place partly in response to the funding councils' assessment of colleges, equal-opportunities policies and the requirement that they produce appropriate guidelines. While progress in this important area has undoubtedly been made, there is still a long way to go: as a 1990–91 HMI report pointed out, while many colleges have successfully used their staff development programmes to raise staff awareness in this area, they still need to pay greater attention to the relationship between the curriculum and equal opportunities and to employ appropriate teaching and learning strategies.[28]

The third group of students in further education with particular requirements are those with disabilities and learning difficulties. With few exceptions, they have had to fight very hard for their rights over the years and although, as we have seen in a previous chapter, local authorities have for some time had a duty to make provision for students with special needs, aged 16 to 19, it was not until the 1992 Further and Higher Education Act that colleges were required 'to have regard for students with learning difficulties'. Precisely how many students with special needs are studying in the further education institutions it is impossible to say. However, a 1986 survey undertaken by Skill (the National Bureau for Students with Disabilities) estimated that there were about 30,000 of them. At present, the FEFC is working on the assumption that they number 100,000; the considerable increase reflects the facts that college rolls have risen considerably, sixth-form colleges are now included in the further education sector, and generally there is a better understanding of their needs.[29] Well before the passing of the 1992 Act, most colleges were devoting substantial resources to this area of work and continue to do so. Some colleges, for example, have a special education sector or appoint a special needs coordinator to oversee the provision of programmes for people with learning difficulties who have been to special schools, who have had support in mainstream schools, or who have attended a local authority day centre. A small number of colleges also cater for students with complex and profound learning difficulties. Courses are commonly available on both a full-time and a part-time basis and students are usually taught in small groups and, where possible, in properly equipped accommodation. Among the courses provided are those aimed to increase confidence and independence, to continue basic education, to enable students to become involved in community service and, last but not least, to prepare them for work. Since becoming independent of their local authorities, some colleges have increased their provision of vocational training for disadvantaged students, both strengthening their involvement with their local communities and also bringing in additional income. There is also a growing recognition of the importance of courses which lead to employment, and over the last few years the FEU has produced a number of useful and informative publications.[30] However, there are still gaps and a degree of duplication in the provision that is made for learners with disabilities and learning difficulties and access to further education still depends on where individuals live and the nature of their disabilities.

Since the passing of the 1992 Act, colleges in England and Wales have been required to include in their strategic plans details of their intended provision for special needs students. Then, towards the end of 1993, the FEFC established a committee, under the chairmanship of Professor John Tomlinson, director of the University of Warwick Institute of Education, to examine the provision of educational opportunities in the colleges for disadvantaged students. In February 1994, the committee, which has a three-year lifespan, announced the launching of the first-ever national enquiry into the special needs of students in English further education institutions: as part of the enquiry, it will attempt to define more closely the term 'special needs'. Clearly, if it includes students who have not done well at school and adult under-achievers who are seeking a second chance, then the number of people with 'special needs' could be as many as 25 per cent of a college population.[31] In addition, the enquiry will as a matter of priority examine the present funding regime for special needs provision, which is regarded as inadequate in that it penalizes colleges which seek to introduce new ways of providing for their disadvantaged students.

Finally, as we have seen, the great majority of colleges make separate provision for their special needs students, who are catered for by units separate from the main body of the college. This way of organizing and delivering programmes has not met with universal approval and has been described by one critic as 'well-intentioned but not well-informed', on the grounds that the negative practice of labelling and segregating groups with assumed 'learning difficulties' devalues the individuals and the activities they are engaged in.[32] It is contended that, in many colleges, little attempt is made to adapt existing mainstream curricula, to change teaching methods to meet individual needs, and to ensure progression from a segregated to a mainstream course. While this may well be true, radical changes have considerable resource and managerial implications which while being tackled by some colleges, other colleges will find it difficult to come to terms with.

Students aged 14 to 16

There are two other groups of students in the colleges whose numbers have grown or are about to do so, those in the 14 to 16 age group and those undertaking courses of higher education. Although further education is officially defined as provision for persons over the compulsory school-leaving age, the colleges have made some provision for the 14 to 16 age group for some years, for example through former 'link courses' in which school-based children spent, say, a day a week in the colleges, and through TVEI schemes to which the colleges contributed. Then, somewhat unexpectedly in October 1993, the FEFC announced that under the terms of the 1992 Act colleges were free to recruit students between the ages of 14 to 16, provided the requirements of the National Curriculum were satisfied and that programmes were suitable to their age, aptitude and ability. Apparently, a number of colleges had already began to recruit under-16s by this time, their numbers running into several thousands. However, opinions within the colleges differ sharply about the wisdom of recruiting students of this age. Some colleges were doubtful of their ability to fulfil the requirements of the National Curriculum, while others were worried about the lack of suitable pastoral support and appropriate sports facilities.[33] On the other hand, students in schools who lack interest and motivation might find a technical or vocational course in the more adult environment of the college much more to their liking. What is indisputable, however, is that the already blurred lines of distinction between secondary schools and the colleges are becoming ever more so. One consequence of this initiative is that there is likely to be keen competition between schools and colleges to recruit 14- to 16-year-olds, as there already is for those aged 16 to 18. It is clearly important that such recruitment should be based on the best interests of the students and the wishes of them and their parents, and not on crude market forces.

Students in Higher Education

Further education colleges have long offered a number of courses, if always comprising a minority of their provision, which come under the heading of higher education, or, as it used to be called, advanced further education (AFE), that is courses of a standard above GCE A-level or its vocational equivalent. This is still the case today, and a glance at the prospectus of, say, a large urban college reveals a substantial number of BTEC Higher National Diploma and Certificate courses, diplomas in management studies and the like, on offer. However, in the past three or four years there has been a substantial development of 'franchised' courses, which in some of the colleges has led to a considerable increase in the number of higher education students. Franchising is an arrangement with a university, usually in the region in which the college is located, whereby the local college delivers the first year of a three-year first degree course, or other programme of higher education, which is validated by the university in question. On the successful completion of the first year at the college, the student then transfers to the university for the other two years. This arrangement has proved attractive to both parties concerned: to the colleges because it promotes recruitment and brings in funding, and also because of what Palmer describes as 'the more covert aim of adding status to individuals and the college collectively';[34] and to the university because it relieves some of the pressure on the growth in student numbers and the shortage of teachers and facilities. Initially, these courses were welcomed by the government and the funding councils as an important means of widening access. They are funded by the higher education funding councils (HEFCs), which give the money to the universities who in turn pass on a share of it, usually about 25 per cent, to the colleges. As a result of government approval and college enthusiasm, franchised course have grown rapidly and in the past few years student numbers have increased from about 10,000 in 1991 to probably nearly 40,000 in 1994. However, from the beginning of the 1994–95 session a sharp financial brake was placed on student recruitment. Following the announcement in the November 1993 budget of the cutting of tuition fees, as part of the government freeze on higher education numbers, the Higher Education Funding Council for England (HEFC) announced in June 1994 that severe financial penalties would be placed on colleges who had expanded their higher education programmes in the 1992–93 and 1993–94 sessions. The upshot is that many colleges will be recruiting few, if any, new students for 1994–95. Concern has also been expressed that the quality control exercised by some of the validating universities has not been all it should be, and there are doubts whether some colleges have sufficiently able staff and the necessary resources to teach effectively at first degree level. However, a recent report from the HEFC entitled *Some aspects of higher education programmes in further education colleges*[35] concludes that on the whole the franchising of courses to the colleges has worked reasonably well and that students have generaly benefited from them. It comments that some of the quality assurance procedures are complex and bureaucratic and that a limited form of validation, whereby the further education colleges implement their own curricula and undertake their own student assessment, might be more effective. Overall, there is no doubt that franchised degree courses are of considerable benefit in that they give access to higher education to students who, for financial or social reasons, can only avail themselves of provision near their homes. For this reason alone, it seems that, financial and quality assurance problems notwithstanding, franchised courses are here to stay.

Support Services

These include guidance and learner support systems, services provided by students' unions, and chaplaincy services. Until fairly recently, further education could fairly be described as 'traditionally, the sector of education in which guidance has been least well developed'.[36] However, in recent years there has been a growing recognition of its importance. One reason for its neglect in the past is the assumption on the part of some colleges that students who have chosen specific vocational courses have already decided on their choice of career and so need no guidance. While this may or may not have been the case, the increase in non-vocational courses and of those concerned with giving a broad introduction to an area of work have made the need for careers guidance pressing and, indeed, many courses of these kinds do include it. The same is true of the increasing number of modular courses and of credit accumulation schemes, which face students with a range of choices and the need to make often difficult decisions about devising appropriate programmes of study. But it is not just in the area of career guidance that students need help; as we have seen, the drop-out rate in further education is unacceptably high, and undoubtedly more learner support would help to raise completion rates. An effective guidance system must also take into account the different needs of disparate groups of students, including school leavers, adults, those from ethnic minorities, and those with disabilities. Some impetus towards encouraging colleges to provide adequate guidance services is given by the DFE's *Charter for Further Education*,[37] which recommends, among other things, that would-be students should be able to turn to the colleges for pre-entry counselling and diagnosis, for assistance with personal difficulties, whether financial or related to accommodation, and that students towards the end of their courses should have access to advice on future career opportunities.

Colleges have, of course, long provided counselling and careers advice, even though it has not always been sufficient either in quality or quantity. Virtually all colleges provide some form or other of both confidential personal counselling and specialist careers advice, though quite large colleges may only have one or two counsellors for the whole student body. Some recent examples of what it calls 'threshold services', or high-profile guidance facilities, are given in a recent FEU publication.[38] These include the provision of a full-scale customer services unit at Croydon College, a student service unit at Hartlepool College, and an adult guidance service at South Hertfordshire College. The FEU is producing a series of bulletins on guidance and learner support, the first of which appeared at the end of 1993 and provided a detailed checklist of learner needs under the headings of the three main stages at which students are likely to need guidance: before entering college, while on courses, and on leaving college.[39] It has also undertaken a national survey of guidance in colleges and produced a report, published in October 1994, *Managing the delivery of guidance in colleges*.[40] Finally, the Royal Society of Arts (RSA) published a leaflet in 1993 recommending the establishment of a National Advisory Council for Careers and Educational Guidance, whose role would initially be advisory. Once properly established it would, among other things, commission research into aspects of guidance, receive and investigate complaints by users of guidance services, 'kitemark' good practice in guidance, and maintain a register of kitemarked agencies.

For a variety of reasons, mainly historical, students' unions in further education colleges have been less well provided for and for the most part still play a less significant part in the lives of students than do their counterparts in higher education. There are several reasons for this state of affairs. Firstly, as the majority of students in the colleges are attending on a part-time basis, commonly for one day a week or in the evenings, they have less need for their services and are less inclined to call upon them. Moreover, their principal affiliation is to their place of work rather than to the college and its students' union. Secondly, as a high proportion of college students are in the 16 to 19 age group, and therefore to a degree *in statu pupilari*, local authorities in the past and the colleges today have not felt obliged to provide the sorts of facilities found in students' unions in higher education institutions. Thirdly, the unions receive a smaller proportion of their funds from the public purse. As many further education students are part-time or even when full-time are not in receipt of discretionary awards, they have to pay their students' union fees on enrolment out of their own pockets, whereas for higher education students, the great majority of whom are on mandatory grants, the fees are in effect paid for by the LEAs.

Nevertheless, as the numbers of full-time students as well as those over the age of 19 in the colleges have increased, so the role of the students' unions has grown. They fulfil at least three important functions for students: they provide a social centre which cuts across the departmental and other college boundaries; they offer opportunities for some students to take part in discussions and contribute to decisions on matters affecting their own colleges and others, regionally and nationally; and of course they provide an advice and support service for students. Many student unions are affiliated to the National Union of Students, which, although the majority of its members are in higher education institutions, does attempt to look after and represent the interests of its members in the further education sector. To this end it issued in July 1993 its response to the DFE's *Charter for Further Education*,[41] in which it both criticizes the Charter for laying undue stress on the 16 to 19 age group at the expense of the rising proportion of full-time and part-time mature students entering further education, and also makes a number of proposals designed to assist students on entry, while on course, and on leaving their colleges. It also comments adversely on the overall inadequacy of the level of financial support available to further education students.

After a lengthy and, at times, acrimonious debate, both within further and higher education and in political circles, legislation was eventually enacted in mid-1994 which, among other things, allows students to opt out of membership of their students' union, How many students will take up this option and what effect it will have on students' unions and their funds remain to be seen. For those who do decide to opt out, it is the government's intention that they should not be disadvantaged by being denied the services available to their fellow students who are members of students' unions. Just how this would operate in practice and what sort of alternative services their colleges could afford to provide for them are open to question. The further education colleges are more likely to be affected by what promises to become a legal minefield than the universities, as a higher percentage of their students are not actively involved in students' unions and are therefore more likely to opt out.

Another area in which further education colleges are less well provided for than higher education is in the provision of chaplaincy services. In all, there are only 240 chaplains of all the Christian denominations, of whom only 40 are part-time, spread among the 470 or so colleges in England and Wales. It is scarcely surprising that in this respect, as in some others, further education has long been the 'Cinderella service'.[42] One of the major reasons for this state of affairs was that the churches assumed that most further education students were living at home and would be adequately served by their home parishes. As the nature of the colleges has changed in this respect, so have attitudes within the churches, and more and more chaplains are being appointed. Ecumenical chaplaincies are becoming increasingly common, some of them being multi-faith, including non-Christian religions such as Judaism, Islam and Hinduism.

Finally, and in some ways most importantly, the support which an increasing number of students need most is financial. As we have pointed out, while most grants for study in further education colleges are discretionary, these are declining in number and value as local authorities' budgets are increasingly stretched. As a consequence, many students find considerable difficulty in funding themselves, a state of affairs which attracts much less public concern than the plight of similarly placed students in higher education. In some cases, they turn for help to their colleges, some of whom devote as much as 3 or 4 per cent of their annual budgets to hardship funds of one sort or another which are supplemented by so-called 'access' funds for full-time students over the age of 19 from the DFE, while others have helped students to raise money from charity.[43] This is hardly a satisfactory state of affairs and the secretary of state has been called upon, by the Association for Colleges among others, to commission a study of the present system of student support.

Notes and References

1   'How to build Big Brother', *Times Educational Supplement*, FE Extra, October, 1993.
2   See,for example, Further Education Funding Council for Wales, *Further Education Statistical Bulletin, 27 July 1992*, Cardiff, FEFCW, Annex A.
3   A. Utley, 'Stricter rules to end FE "fiddle"', *Times Higher Educational Supplement*, 8 July 1994, p. 40.
4   Department for Education, *The New Qualifications Framework*, London, DFE, March 1994.
5   'League tables', *EDUCA*, **131**, 3 (1993).
6   City and Guilds, *Annual Report 1992–93*, London, City and Guilds, p. 9.
7   *EDUCA*, **131** (1993).
8   Audit Commission/OFSTED, *Unfinished Business: Full-time Educational Courses for 16–19 Year Olds*, London, Audit Commission, 1993.
9   'Staying on or dropping out?', *FEU Newsletter*, April 1994, p. 8.
10   Business and Technology Council, *Staying the Course*, London, BTEC, 1993.
11   Audit Commission/OFSTED, *Unfinished Business: Full-time Educational Courses for 16–19 Year Olds, op. cit.*
12   'Vocational A Level bursting the banks', *Times Higher Educational Supplement*, 8 July 1994, pp. 1 and 40.
13   HMI, *Education for Adults*, London, HMSO, 1991, p. 2.
14   *Ibid.*
15   Further Education Unit, *Paying Their Way: The Experiences of Adult Leavers in Vocational Education and Training in FE Colleges*, London, FEU, 1993, p. 5.
16   D. Tyler, 'Adult education: now the good news', *Guardian Education*, 23 November 1993, p. 7.
17   J. O'Leary, 'Never too old to learn', *Times*, 9 May 1994, p. 31.
18   P. Wilson, 'Home of deserving courses', *Times Educational Supplement*, Further Education Update, 2 December 1994, p. 15.
19   Reported in *EDUCA*, **134**, 2 (1993).
20   M. Woodrow and L. Simms, *Education Years and Access Courses*, London, University of North London, 1993.
21   F. Reeves *et al.*, *Community Need and Further Education: The Practice of Community-centred Education at Bilston Community College*, Bilston, Education Now, 1993, pp. 43–4.
22   Ibid., p. 7.
23   I. Nash, 'Cash row endangers jobless plan', *Times Educational Supplement*, 15 October, 1993, p. 3.
24   Further Education Unit, *Paying Their Way: The Experiences of Adult Leavers in Vocational Education and Training in FE Colleges*, London, FEU, 1993, p. 18.
25   HMI, *Education for Adults*, London, HMSO, 1991, p. 18.
26   Further Education Unit, *Ethnic Monitoring and its Uses in Colleges*, London, FEU, 1992.
27   Department For Education, *Statistical Bulletin, 26/93*, London, DFE, December 1993, Table 13.

28 Department for Education, *Assessing Achievement*, London, DFE, 1991.
29 I. Nash, 'A national special needs survey at last', *Times Educational Supplement*, 4 February 1994, p. 8.
30 See, for example, Further Education Unit, *Transition into Employment*, Bulletins 1 and 2, FEU, 1991 and 1992, and *Developing Competence: Guidelines on Implementing Provision Leading to Employment-Led Qualifications for Learners with Disabilities and Learning Difficulties*, London, FEU, 1993.
31 I. Nash, 'A national special needs survey at last', *Times Educational Supplement*, 4 February 1994, p. 8.
32 J. Whittaker, 'Rhetoric removed from reality', *Times Educational Supplement*, 14 January 1994, p. 7.
33 I. Nash, 'Colleges to recruit under-16s', *Times Educational Supplement*, October 1993.
34 A. Palmer, 'Franchised degree teaching – what can education learn from business?', *Journal of Higher and Further Education*, **16**, (3) (1992), p. 83.
35 Higher Education Funding Council for England, *Some aspects of higher education programmes in further education colleges*, London, HEFCE, 1994.
36 T. Watts, *Briefing Paper for the National Commission on Education*, London, NCE, October 1993.
37 Department for Education/Welsh Office, *The Charter for Further Education*, London/Cardiff, DFE/Welsh Office, 1993.
38 Further Education Unit, *Flexible Colleges*, London, FEU, Part 1, Priorities for Action, n.d., p. 37.
39 Further Education Unit, *Learners Needs in College Based Guidance*, London, FEU, 1993.
40 Further Education Unit, *Managing the Delivery of Guidance in Colleges*, London, FEU, October 1994.
41 National Union of Students, *NUS Response to the DFE Charter for Further Education*, London, NUS, July 1993.
42 P. Kingston, 'The Lord is My Shepherd', *Guardian Education*, 28 June 1994, p. 4.
43 I. Nash, 'Student hardship funds rocketing', *Times Educational Supplement*, 14 October 1994, p. 6.

Five

The Management of Further Education Colleges

Further education colleges have become increasingly complex institutions to manage. In terms of 'product lines', the largest of them resemble the variety offered by a medium-sized supermarket, but one which produces, markets, finances and tests its own products, and deals with many thousands of customers. Among the smallest, however, are the sixth-form colleges which may run a relatively narrow range of courses for mainly full-time students and would probably reject any such comparison with commercial or industrial management models. As we have seen, the legislative framework within which the colleges operate is contained in two Acts of Parliament which have not altogether ironed out the differences between them.

The 1988 Education Reform Act began the process of reforming college governing bodies by specifying the maximum number of governors and the broad composition of the boards. Since the definition of a further education college in the Act excluded those which did not provide part-time education 'to a significant extent', the sixth-form colleges were not at this stage included. The main objective of the Act's provisions concerning governing bodies was to increase the influence over colleges of representatives of local industry and commerce, and to reduce the impact of the local authorities. Of the total of not more than 25 governors, at least half were to be drawn from industry and not more than 20 per cent were to be local education authority (LEA) members or nominees. Some colleges, keen to streamline their often unwieldy governing bodies, reduced the number of their governors to around twenty. Many of them were encouraged by their industry and business mentors to adopt a style of working similar to that of an industrial board of directors, rather than the elected council, from which they were now expected to distance themselves.

A college governing body has indeed some unique features. It operates under the terms of its Instrument, giving the constitution of the governing body, and its Articles, which determine its conduct. Under the 1988 Act these were to be established by the LEA and approved by the Secretary of State, who then acquired the right to amend them. The Act also established arrangements for the appointment of industry governors which rapidly became unworkable, and were therefore reformed in the 1992 legislation. Technically, the LEA was to appoint the governors, but local and national bodies were to be nominated as the source of appointees, with the nominating bodies themselves to be approved by the governors or the Secretary of State. This led to some convoluted arrangements, with 'search committees' set up either to hunt for suitable people, or to ensure that there was some continuity with existing governing bodies by identifying organizations which could be relied upon to make appropriate nominations.

The governing body as established under the 1988 Act did not carry any liability for financial loss, since its operation was supervised by the LEA. At the same time, however, the Act required LEAs to devise schemes of financial delegation by which the bulk of their funds for further education would pass to the colleges themselves, in much the same way as they were starting to do for schools. The intention was to ensure that no more than 15 per cent of the block grant for further education made available by the government would be retained for central LEA services. This led to some lively debates between colleges and their LEAs, since it was by no means clear in all cases what constituted the grant aid for further education, or how the money had historically been spent. Jokes about window-boxes for town halls apart, there were some serious casualties of these arrangements. It became apparent, for instance, that in some LEAs arrangements which enabled schoolchildren to attend courses run by their local colleges, and regarded as an important feature of the transition from school to work, had been doubly funded, from both the schools' and colleges' budgets. Once the finances were clarified and schools were required to pass funds to colleges for such courses, many of them ceased. As a consequence, the number of these courses declined substantially between 1990 and 1992; however, a survey which reported in April 1994[1] suggests that schools may now be finding ways to purchase them again. Student transport, where college students shared the same buses as schoolchildren, caused some similar problems, as did the education of students with learning disabilities, funding for whose courses was often shared between special schools or social services and colleges. When the changes in these funding arrangements threatened to result in substantially increased costs, college governing bodies found themselves drawn into the planning of course provision. In the main, however, college governors make use of their right to delegate powers to the principal and senior management of the college. These powers generally extend to the appointment of all but the most senior staff, the details of course planning, and other matters linked to the day-to-day running of the college. While these powers of delegation have not changed following the most recent legislation, there are some important new safeguards.

Meanwhile, no sooner had college governors and managements become accustomed to the arrangements determined by the 1988 Act with their schemes of delegation of financial powers from LEAs, than they were faced with the arrangements established by the Further and Higher Education Act of 1992. As we have seen, under its provisions the further education colleges, together with sixth-form colleges, have become independent corporations, receiving their funds from the funding councils. Governors started to prepare for their new corporate status in late 1992, in order for it to take effect from 1 April 1993, referred to as 'vesting day'. The major change to governing bodies effected by the 1992 Act was to slim them down further and to increase once more the representation from industry and commerce. All existing governors would become initial members of the new 'corporations', unless they were nominated and appointed by an LEA, or employees of an LEA (excepting teachers), or elected by an LEA. This effectively broke the existing links between colleges and their former LEAs, although some local authority nominees crept back onto corporations as co-opted members with a local community interest. While some principals were delighted to be completely free of LEAs at last, others recognized the value of the support of local authority members and felt their loss most keenly. At its first meeting, the corporation was to determine its eventual membership, within a band of numbers between 10 and 20.[2] There was to be a further increase in members representing industry and business, and there could be staff and student members and co-options from the community or special interest groups. In addition, there had to be a representative from the local Training and Enterprise Council (TEC). Appointments to membership of the corporations are made by the other members, with none of the previous accountability to the bodies from which they are drawn, although staff and student members tend to be appointed as a result of elections from their constituencies. A survey of governing bodies before and after incorporation by the Further Education Staff College[3] (FESC) showed a distinct reduction in the number of governors with a direct interest in eduation, as well as a significant reduction in the number of women members.

The 1992 Act transferred responsibility for funding the sector to the funding councils, and required that the colleges give them the information needed to do their work. LEAs and any other institution to which they gave financial support had to do the same. As school sixth forms were excluded from the new sector, but at the same time were given the opportunity to run further education courses and recruit part-time students, including adults, this did not make for efficient planning at the local level. Common articles of government of the colleges were published giving their boards of governors responsibility for: determining their educational character and mission; overseeing their activities; the effective and efficient use of their resources; ensuring their solvency; safeguarding their assets, which were taken over from their LEAs on vesting day; approving annual budgets; appointing senior staff; and setting the framework for the pay and conditions of the staff. The principal of the college became the chief executive and was given specific delegated responsibilities for educational planning, budgetary control, and student discipline. There was still to be an academic board, drawn from the students and staff, responsible for advising the chief executive on specific matters relevant to the academic work of the college. Although the precise law determining the responsibilities and liabilities of governors is still dependent on the interpretation given by courts in particular cases, they had been advised to ensure that any course of action proposed by the college should be in accordance with its articles of government, or trust deed if there were a relevant charity. In addition, they should not bind their colleges to actions they could not implement, they should allow colleges to continue to operate if they became insolvent, they should act honestly and reasonably, taking professional advice where necessary, and they should avoid personal conflicts of interest.[4] The earliest circulars from the Further Education Funding Council for England (FEFC) added further advice on the administrative arrangements and financial safeguards expected from colleges – for example, the governors were expected to appoint an internal audit committee to advise them – as well as arrangements for strategic planning, property management, personnel management, and so on. Management consultants contracted from the private sector also gave advice on preparing for incorporation,[5] and on other matters. Initially, there was some difficulty over a misreading of guidance from the Department for Education (DFE), which appeared to allow governors to receive allowances for their services, but about a year after incorporation the FEFC declared that despite the heavy responsibilities incurred by chairs of boards of governors and of their sub-committees, they could only receive legal payments for expenses and not for loss of earnings or honoraria. In May 1994, the FEFC issued a succinct, comprehensive and authoritative document, entitled *Guide for College Governors*, which is a full account of the workings of the further education sector. Although written from the point of view of the college governor, much of it is of general interest and is very informative about how further education operates.[6] It, too, stated explicitly that payments to college governors, apart from travel and subsistence costs, were illegal and reinforced this policy by introducing new account rules which obliged auditors to check if payments had been made. The effect of this ruling was to oblige more than 100 colleges who had been making payments to members of their governing bodies to stop doing so. However, a number of college principals have criticized the FEFC's diktat on the grounds that it will make it more difficult to recruit good governors, particularly chairmen, and that it will militate against the appointment of, for example, people in lower-paid jobs who find it difficult to obtain time off from work with pay in order to attend board meetings. Consequently, the Colleges' Employers' Forum (CEF) has asked the Secretary of State for Education to review the situation sympathetically.

At the end of 1994, two cases became public which highlighted the difficulties that can arise between determined boards of governors and the oversight of the funding councils. In the first instance, conflict between governors and staff at Wilmorton Tertiary College, Derby, led the FEFC to appoint a committee of enquiry which published its report in November 1994. Pulling no punches, it concluded that the governing body had managed its business in a deplorable way and had failed to control the authoritarian and erratic behaviour of the principal, who had resigned some months earlier. The second case was that of St Philip's Sixth Form College, in Birmingham, a Roman Catholic college whose staff and parents strongly objected to the governors' proposal to close the college on the grounds that as it now serves a mixed local community including many Muslims, Hindus, and Sikhs, Catholic students constitute just under a third of the student body. A report of a committee of enquiry on the actions of the governing body, also published in November 1994, found the governors directly responsible for the mismanagement of the college's affairs. Consequently, the chief executive of the FEFC has recommended to the Secretary of State that the governing bodies of the two institutions be reconstituted and, at the time of writing, her decisions are being awaited.

Meanwhile, in the year or so following incorporation, college principals had mixed feelings about the severance of links with the LEAs, while the latter were more usually aggrieved to have lost valuable assets and influence. In the run-up to incorporation, the Education Assets Board which had been set up when the polytechnics were taken out of local authority control a few years before, was given the task of overseeing disputes between colleges and LEAs about which property the former should inherit. In due course, these disagreements were overcome, often leaving the LEAs feeling the aggrieved party, even though much of the property taken over by the colleges was not in good condition. Indeed, a survey of the state of college buildings commissioned by the FEFC and published in March 1994 estimated that if they were to be brought up to scratch, £839 million of capital investment would be required, including £359 million to meet essential health and safety requirements. Given the cost of meeting these capital projects deriving from before incorporation, it is unlikely that there will be any money made available for new buildings for some considerable time.

To sum up the changes that flowed from the 1992 Act, the major differences for the colleges were that, legally, they had become corporations run by chief executives; they were responsible for managing their own finances and for instituting the required financial controls and auditing; they now employed their own staff; and they owned their own premises and were responsible for their maintenance and development. Given their new circumstances, the colleges rapidly set up structures to oversee their finances. In many cases, this resulted in the old-style registrar, or in the case of sixth-form colleges the bursar, being replaced by a director of finance, often recruited from industry or the former polytechnics who, having gone through a similar process themselves a few years earlier, provided much useful experience and advice about the transition to incorporated status. The need to pay close attention to financial affairs and the resulting creation of specialist posts caused some re-thinking of other management functions in colleges. For some years, growing numbers of college principals had been reviewing and revising the roles and responsibilities of their staff, especially those at senior level. The national pay agreement of 1990 had established 'management spine' posts with very different conditions of employment from those of main-grade lecturers. This enabled college principals to institute working practices for senior management staff which were different from those who were mainly lecturing. In addition, for a number of reasons the role of the traditional heads of department, the so-called 'barons of further education', had increasingly come under scrutiny. Firstly, the character of the work of many colleges was changing quickly, in response to industrial and demographic shifts: for example, some departments like business and general education were growing fast, while others like building construction and mining were declining steeply, if indeed they survived at all. Secondly, it became apparent that many heads of department were duplicating each others' work in different contexts, while important cross-college functions lacked attention. Thirdly, the colleges were increasingly under pressure from government to respond to its demands to become more efficient, more effective and more competitive.

Whether because it was simply the opportunity for a principal, especially a new one, to make a mark on a college, or for more fundamental, functional reasons, it became commonplace for colleges to be reorganized. Thus, it is now common to find a directorate of senior staff dealing with functional responsibilities like finance, personnel, resources, marketing, curriculum, and student affairs, with heads of subject areas handling the running of courses at the next level down. One year after incorporation, a review of the situation noted a rise in management posts in colleges, accompanied by flatter structures, that is with fewer hierarchical layers, and greater accountability among line managers for targets and performance.[7] At the same time, there is an increase in 'hybrid' posts which combine academic and non-academic duties, on different salary scales from those of lecturers, and a general increase in the ratio of support staff to lecturers. Reflecting the impact which changing demands had had on the principals themselves, the Association of Principals of Colleges (APC) recorded that no fewer than 44 per cent of them had left their posts during the period between the two education acts.[8] Many withdrew to avoid what they regarded as unacceptable changes to their traditional roles and because of trepidation about the demands of the new sector and their own lack of training.[9] The main challenges were expected to be the management of reduced budgets, problems with their LEAs over the changeover to funding council control, and carrying their staff with them through the changes ahead. An example of a serious dispute which has occurred between colleges and a local authority over the handing over of assets at the time of incorporation became public at the end of 1994, when two colleges in the West Midlands began a case in the High Court in London against Birmingham City Council. The colleges claim that the authority illegally kept back money from the European Social Fund which should have been used for the benefit of their students and was also unjustified in clawing back money which it alleges the colleges overspent while under its control.

Meanwhile, the setting up of the funding councils was a further step on the road to making colleges responsible for the quality and efficiency of their own provision. Before that, however, a number of other organizations had been involved in this process. In June 1985, for example, the Audit Commission, established to advise on ways of getting better value for money from local authority expenditure, produced a report on the further education system, entitled *Obtaining Better Value from Further Education*.[10] It suggested that further education could improve its efficiency by marketing itself better, by improving the ratio of students to staff, by speeding up the process of invoicing internal customers, and by tightening up on non-teaching costs by, for instance, making better use of space. The effects created by this report on the colleges together with the local activities of district auditors, who could scrutinize college affairs, led to considerable improvements in their efficiency and effectiveness over the next decade and prompted many of the managerial changes referred to above. These improvements took various forms. Firstly, the colleges gave more attention to the creation of computerized management information systems (MIS), the first of which had appeared in the early 1970s, but which had been slow to develop, mainly through lack of a properly coordinated approach which would make best use of the available resources. The DFE helped to finance a system developed at the FESC, known as FEMIS (Further Education Management Information System). Established in 1984, it became a commercial concern, taken up by perhaps half of all colleges. Other systems were developed by LEAs in conjunction with computer manufacturers and software houses, and the market eventually shook down to two or three major systems. The expense of establishing such systems was partly offset by specific grants from the DFE, but even now few colleges have developed really streamlined systems which make the best use of modern technology. As a survey conducted by the London and South Eastern Regional Advisory Council (LASER), published in 1993, showed, many colleges in its region had inadequate information technology systems for effective management.[11] Hardware costs have been one obstacle and lack of management commitment another. To manage such systems properly has taken expertise which has needed to be bought in to colleges at considerable expense, and there has been some reluctance to divert resources on such a scale in order to measure efficiency, when the effectiveness of the college might be improved by expenditure elsewhere. Such reluctance has probably finally been dispelled by the demands of the funding councils for proper financial and other forms of resource control, and few colleges are now managing without an appropriately qualified resources director and a team of information managers. Without such arrangements, it will be very difficult for colleges to obtain the resources they need from the funding councils as the resourcing models for colleges are not simple. The Further Education Unit (FEU) reported in autumn 1994 that there was an observable shift in attitudes towards greater use of sophisticated management systems. Indeed, according to the FEU,[12] the attitude of colleges towards the installation of computerized MIS is changing. Helped by improvements in computer software and the technology of data collection, more and more colleges now accept the need for an appropriate and accessible system which, among other things, can keep track of students on modular programmes, record the use of training credits, determine the profile of the college population, and enhance support for adult students progressing from uncertificated courses to those leading to qualifications.

At an early stage, the FEFC embarked upon an elaborate consultation with colleges about the various methods of funding which might be established. Its consultative document, *Funding Learning*,[13] issued in December 1992, is both an intelligent analysis of the sector and also a proposal for six different ways in which funding might be managed. After consultation, the new sector opted for perhaps the most imaginative, and certainly the least simple, of all the options. As we have seen, this was a method of funding based on units of provision, which took into account the need to guide students carefully through their initial choice of study programmes, teach them consistently, and help them to achieve their ultimate qualification aim, or other equally satisfactory outcome. It was a bold move, which is certainly testing to the limit the MIS of colleges. It is a student-centred solution, which recognizes that learners have individual objectives, as opposed to the more suspect tradition of filling seats in classrooms until the statistical returns are completed in November, and not paying too much attention to what happens to the learners after that. Under the new system there is an important set of relationships between student guidance and choice of programme, the retention of students on programmes, and the achievement of satisfactory results. If any one of the elements fails, there is an adverse effect on the funding received by the college. The FEFC has also established a tariff committee to advise on ways of sharing out the finite amount of money available to it in order to encourage the system to move in particular ways. For instance, as we have seen in the face of a sudden decline in part-time job-related education, it has produced some tariffs which might provide an incentive to more energetic developments in this field. The system is reasonably sensitive and can be used on a yearly basis to reflect trends or to steer the system in the direction of particular targets. If nothing else, it will keep college staff responsible for marketing and planning on their toes.

The development of more sophisticated systems of resource control has been one way in which the colleges have responded to outside pressures. The improvement of marketing has been another, again encouraged by the Audit Commission, and by the DFE, Employment Department (ED), and the Department of Trade and Industry (DTI). The Audit Commission identified a wasteful duplication of resources in many aspects of post-16 education, with schools and colleges vying with each other for the same group of students. However, it pointed out that as the participation rate, especially of young people in full-time education and training, improved, so resources would be better utilized. As we have seen, this indeed happened as the number of 16- to 19-year-olds staying on in full-time education and training after the end of compulsory schooling dramatically increased in the early 1990s. This was due in part to the efforts of the colleges, assisted to some extent by the DFE, which produced publicity materials aimed at young people, to improve their image and their communications with potential students. A major project funded by the ED was 'The Responsive College' project, managed from Coombe Lodge, the FESC, which was influential in changing attitudes and practices in colleges towards a sharper focus on the needs of the students and those who sponsored them. Another interesting initiative was the PICKUP (Professional, Industrial and Commercial Updating) programme which ran for 10 years from 1983 to 1993. Its aim was to encourage colleges to identify and to respond to the need to update skills among the working population and to bring in revenue by providing industry and business with tailor-made short courses, paid for by employers with grant aid from the DES. PICKUP was sufficiently successful for the DFE to propose the closure of the programme in 1993 on the supposition that its objectives were now fully accepted by the colleges. There has certainly been an improvement in the image most colleges offer to the outside world. Prospectuses and other written information have been redesigned, special short course centres have been established, with high-quality facilities designed to be attractive to adult, paying customers, and courses now tend to be offered over an extended period of the year, with flexible start dates. In addition, a number of colleges have increased significantly their provision of short courses which are designed specifically to meet the needs of industry and their employees. Among them, for example, are colleges which have successfully moved away from traditional short course provision in favour of tailor-made personal development programmes to update and enhance the skills and qualifications of employees in local industry; and agricultural colleges, which offer a wide range of specialist short courses to meet the specific needs of the industries they serve, in such subject areas as agriculture, animal care, health and safety, food and dairy technology and management. The appointment by many colleges of marketing directors was another change to senior management teams which reflects changing circumstances and attitudes towards recruiting students and designing the kind of programmes they said they wanted.

Both the government and the funding councils are interested in maximizing the use of college resources to increase the number of people receiving work-related education and training. As we have seen, the FEFC has set a target of a 25 per cent increase in further education student numbers over the first three years of its operation, funded by a 16 per cent increase in resources. This growth, which is related to the national education and training targets, is likely to involve most colleges in increasing their recruitment of adult students. The funding councils have also been very sensitive to the needs of some students who will find it difficult to achieve as highly as their colleagues, and from the beginning they have paid considerable attention to those with special educational needs. They have probably recognized that the crude application of market forces and formula funding could well result in the disappearance of some socially necessary, but expensive, provision in colleges and have therefore gone to some lengths to support the principle that colleges should serve all members of their communities. As a result, the formula for funding provision for students with special needs is sufficiently flexible to cater, for example, for those with the most severe disabilities. In addition, as we have seen, a special committee has been established to advise on the best arrangements for those with special needs in further education, with the power to commission research in support of its work, and is due to report in 1995.

A final category of provision over which a question mark currently hangs is the education of adults. The consequences of the 1992 Further and Higher Education Act were such that provision for adult learners now falls into two categories: courses financed by the funding councils, such as those which lead to vocational qualifications and the acquisition of basic skills; and those courses run mainly for recreational purposes, many of them in the continuing education departments of further education colleges, but also in free-standing adult education colleges and institutes. The latter group of courses remain the responsibility of LEAs, which have had to raise fees to the level which allows them to be self-sustaining. There has been some consequent decline in numbers, and many adult education institutes have been closed or merged with colleges, which have inherited the problem of ensuring that they are adequately financed.

One of the major developments affecting the colleges has been the increasing demand from a variety of sources for quality assurance, that is the introduction of some mechanism to monitor the quality of the courses they offer. The Audit Commission may be said to have begun the debate about efficiency and effectiveness, that is the achievement of results of the required standards within reasonable resources, with the publication in 1985 of its report, *Obtaining Better Value from Further Education*.[14] This issue was pursued in a national report issued two years later by the Department of Education and Science (DES) and the local authority associations, entitled *Managing Colleges Efficiently*,[15] which put forward various performance indicators designed to judge the achievement of students against levels of expenditure. With the establishment of the funding councils, attention has turned to devising formulae which link funding to the quality of college courses. Then, in 1993, the publication of *Unfinished Business*,[16] by the Audit Commission and the Office for Standards in Education (OFSTED), identified the degree of wasted resources caused by student drop-out and wastage and increased the pressure for funding to be linked to student achievement. However, the report had great difficulty in finding a fair basis for comparison between vocational and academic courses.

Industry has, of course, long been concerned to ensure its products are of high quality, and to this end has increasingly introduced quality control measures over the production process and other management systems of checking and auditing. A so-called 'total quality management' system for an industrial concern might demand that all its suppliers were as committed to quality management as it was itself, and these suppliers might include the suppliers of training, among them its local further education colleges. Consequently, one way some colleges have reacted to this situation is to apply available industrial standards to their quality management systems. For this purpose, they turned to the British Standards Institute (BSI), which has devised a system, which complies with international standards, known as BS5750.[17] The purpose of BS5750 is to ensure that a product is consistent with predetermined standards set by the manufacturer, and that these standards are satisfactory to the customer so that few or no complaints result. Although the BSI published guidelines suggesting how its procedures might be applied to education, their introduction into an education institution is fraught with difficulties, not the least of which is how to define its 'product'; for example, is it the students or the courses? In practice, individual colleges have decided for themselves; Sandwell College, in the West Midlands, the first college to lay claim to BSI certification for all its college procedures, defined its product as the improvement in student achievement as the result of being on a course. To this end, it reviewed all its activities to ensure that they were supportive of, and consistent with, the production of good-quality education experiences, and it succeeded in satisfying external auditors that this was the case. However, such a procedure is enormously detailed and time-consuming and needs to be continuously reviewed and audited. In practice, Sandwell and other colleges who have adopted BS5750 have found the maintenance of this level of quality management even more difficult and rigorous than its original implementation. It is hardly surprising, therefore, that most colleges adopting BS5750 procedures have applied them only to limited parts of their provision, such as customized short course units.

While agreeing in principle with the need to ensure high-quality provision, many in the education service have found this linking of quality with product control and economic efficiency distasteful. They have preferred, therefore, to link quality with strategic planning, which in practice has frequently resulted in the introduction of self-assessments by course teams, or departments, of the quality of their provision during a given year, judged against preset criteria. Typically, this requires a system of reporting inside the college, with plans for future improvement where appropriate, generally linked to some aspects of resource allocation. This system of continuous quality improvement adopted or attempted in many colleges imitated some of the features already well established in higher education, often as a part of the accreditation of institutions by bodies such as the Council for National Academic Awards (CNAA), which was responsible for validating degree courses in the former polytechnics. Consequently, colleges which had some experience of offering higher-level awards were among the first to see that these quality assurance systems had benefits to offer to the rest of their programmes. How much improvement these processes bring about in practice is a matter of opinion, but while they undoubtedly have a gargantuan appetite for paper, they do introduce some aspects of critical self-evaluation which are not without benefit to both staff and students.

The further education colleges were, until March 1993, subject to inspection by Her Majesty's Inspectors (HMIs), and to a lesser extent by LEA inspectors, under the same arrangements as the rest of the maintained education system. This meant that from time to time, probably no more than once in ten years, there would be a full inspection of a college's work by HMI, with a published report on the quality of provision. In between, there would be occasional short visits by subject specialists and a degree of monitoring by the HMI general inspector allocated to the college. For the Secretary of State for Education this work of HMI was significant in that it provided information and advice about the further education system. For the colleges, however, it was less clear what the effect of these reporting activities was, except perhaps after a formal general college inspection, when responses to a published report were formally required from colleges and LEAs. This system of inspection by HMI and LEA inspectors has now gone. In its place, the funding councils have set up their own inspection arrangements and LEA inspectors no longer have a role in colleges, except in the limited area of LEA-funded adult education.

As far as the funding councils are concerned, the criteria for their judgements are published in their circulars[18] and the reports of their inspections are published. An innovatory development by comparison with the way in which HMI operated is that a senior member of the college staff is invited to become a member of the inspection team. So far, these changes in inspection procedures and judgements have been designed to ensure their openness, in contrast to the sometimes mysterious operations of HMI. These early efforts by the FEFC appear to have been welcomed by the colleges as supportive; as yet, however, the funding councils have not based their funding of the colleges on judgements of the quality of their provision. There is no doubt that the greater the openness of the inspection procedures and the greater the part the colleges play in them, the more they will wish to become involved in these activities in their own right. Given that the colleges are increasingly involved in improving their own systems of quality control and the fact that external inspection procedures are expensive to operate, it may eventually be the case that the monitoring of quality becomes a matter for the colleges themselves.

Given all the changes that have taken place in the management of colleges in recent years, it might be supposed that their members of staff might have played, and be playing, a significant part in determining policies. However, while the professional associations have certainly made their views known, they have had a relatively limited effect, as have most other trade unions and professional associations affected by employment legislation introduced by successive Conservative governments since 1979. The National Association of Teachers in Further and Higher Education (NATFHE) was for many years not affiliated to the Trades Union Congress (TUC), although as the major staff representative body it took the lead in negotiations on pay and conditions. While taking a political stand on many issues, it maintains special interest groups for teachers of particular subjects, some of which have been highly influential in matters related to curriculum and staff development. The Association of Teachers and Lecturers (ATL) also has members in further education and as we have seen, the sixth-form colleges have their own body in the form of the

Association of Principals of Sixth Form Colleges (APVIC). Teacher representatives on college governing bodies are elected individuals, and may or may not represent the interests of trade unions or professional bodies. There have been significant difficulties in colleges over the expectation that after incorporation staff would transfer to new contracts of employment, either negotiated locally with the college governors, or along the lines of new model contracts suggested by the CEF.

The many changes which have taken place in the further education sector in recent years have in turn greatly changed the role of the senior management teams in the colleges. Senior managers have traditionally arrived at their posts through the familiar route of teaching, followed by experience in a college middle management team, a progression which has not always adequately prepared them for the tasks they now face. While training programmes have been available to them, they have not always regarded them as very effective.[19] Nationally, the FESC has been a major source of expertise and information on the management and government of colleges. However, as we have seen, the FESC, together with the FEU, is to be combined into a single organization to be known as the Further Education Development Agency (FEDA). How effective this new body will be in providing the sorts of training programmes needed by college managers remains to be seen.

Clearly, the tasks of college managers have changed very considerably in the past decade or so. In the words of Ruth Gee, Chief Executive of the Association for Colleges (AfC):

> Pressures to expand, to produce annual efficiency savings, to deliver a more relevant curriculum, to compete yet collaborate, to be answerable to the funding councils, local and national government bodies and to remain responsive to the needs of the local community comprise the everyday challenge colleges have to meet.[20]

In order to respond effectively to this challenge, many colleges have restructured their organizations; introduced new procedures; appointed new senior staff with titles such as 'estate manager', 'director of finance' and 'marketing director'; and have altered their very names and adopted new logos. In the process, they have increasingly adopted the language of business, by, for example, referring to their students as 'clients'. It is hardly surprising, therefore, that a recent survey has found that the priorities of many senior managers have shifted away from the quality of their educational programmes to the development of secure financial and business systems.[21]

Against the background of so much change, colleges increasingly view competition with neighbouring colleges as a waste of time and effort and a few of them have merged either with other colleges or with higher education institutions. Among those that have already done so are Coleg Pencraig in Anglesey and Coleg Gwynedd across the Menai Strait in North Wales, who have come together to form one institution, and Portsmouth College of Arts and Technology, which has merged with the University of Portsmouth. The position of some of the small specialist colleges is also somewhat insecure, as they lack the resources to support the necessary management infrastructure. It is doubtless partly for that reason that the Lincolnshire College of Agriculture and Horticulture and the Lincolnshire College of Art and Design have merged with De Montfort University, Leicester. Finally, at least two further education colleges, the bulk of whose provision is in higher education, are seeking to transfer to the higher education sector. These are the Norwich College of Art and Design and Writtle Agricultural College, Essex. It is a sign of the times that the FEFC has established a 'reorganizations' committee to oversee proposals for mergers and transfer and it seems very likely that in the years ahead more mergers of colleges and transfers to the higher education sector will occur.

Finally, it comes as no surprise that unprecedented numbers of principals of colleges appear to have resigned or retired from their posts at the end of the summer term of 1994.[21] The combined effects upon them of having to retain their traditional responsibility for academic leadership and the delivery of courses, while at the same time taking on new responsibilities for corporate management, are clearly taking their toll. Their new sets of responsibilities, such as those for financial and personnel management and the adoption of new accounting practices, not to mention having to cope with demands for accountability from the funding councils and the government, have put new pressure on already heavily burdened principals. Some principals may have departed because they felt ill-equipped to cope with the changes that have occurred in the running of the colleges and their successors may fare better. Nevertheless, it is undoubtedly the case that administering colleges of further education has become an increasingly complex and stressful business and is scarcely likely to become less so in the next few years.

Notes and References

1   'Further Education Focus', *Times Educational Supplement*, 1 April 1994. A survey to study the reactions of further education colleges to the first year of incorporation.

2   Details are set out in the Education (Government of Further Education Corporations) (Former Further Education Colleges) Regulations 1992, Cmnd 92/1963, London, HMSO.

3   J. Graystone, with W. J. Bayliff, S. Evans and I. Reece, *FE Governors and their contribution to a quality learning service*, Blagdon, FEU/FESC, Research Report RPT16, 1994.

4   Polytechnics and Colleges Funding Council, *Guide for Governors*, London, PCFC, September 1991.

5   For example, *Getting Your College Ready*, London, Touche Ross Management Consultants for FEFC, 1992.
6   Further Education Funding Council, *Guide for College Governors*, Coventry, FEFC, May 1994.
7   L. Turner, Presidential Address to Annual Conference, *NEWSLINK* (Journal of Association of Principals of Colleges), **4**(2) (1993).
8   E. Ashton, 'Management of Change in Further Education: Some Perceptions of College Principals', Unpublished PhD thesis, Loughborough University of Technology, 1995.
9   Ibid.
10 Audit Commission, *Obtaining Better Value from Further Education*, London, Audit Commission, 1985.
11 T. Tysome, 'Colleges do not have vital IT tools', *Times Higher Educational Supplement*, 18 June 1993.
12 'Information strategies in colleges', *FEU Newsletter*, Autumn 1994, p. 6.
13 Further Education Funding Council, *Funding Learning*, Coventry, FEFC, December 1992.
14 Audit Commission, O*btaining Better Value from Further Education*, *op. cit.*
15 Department of Education and Science/Council of Local Education Authorities, *Managing Colleges Efficiently*, London, DES, 1987.
16 Audit Commission/OFSTED, *Unfinished Business: Full-time Educational Courses for 16–19 year olds*, London, Audit Commission, 1993.
17 See British Standards Institute, *BSI Standards Catalogue*, London, Copyright of British Standards, 1994. BS5750 provides guidance on principal quality concepts and on the selection and use of standards on systems of internal quality management and external quality assurance.
18 See, for example, FEFC, *Assessing Achievement*, Circular 93/28, London, FEFC, 1993.
19 Eric Ashton, *op. cit.*
20 R. Gee, 'A year of living dangerously', *Times Educational Supplement,* Further Education Update, 15 April 1994, p. 24.
21 A. Utley, 'Teaching loses out to business', *Times Higher Educational Supplement*, 29 July 1994, p. 4.
22 'Principals quit their jobs as pressures on colleges mount', *FEU Newsletter*, Autumn 1994, p. 6.

Six

Teacher Education, Staff Development and Research into Further Education

As will be clear from the previous chapters, the growing complexity of the further education sector in recent years has placed greater demands and responsibilities on the shoulders of the staff who teach in it. As a consequence, the need for teacher education and staff development has proportionately increased and, like virtually every other aspect of further education, has been the subject of much debate. Both these areas are influenced by research studies into further education, and in the course of this chapter we shall examine teacher education, staff development, and research into further education in detail.

Teacher Education and Training for Further Education

The provision of initial teacher training for further education staff, while not compulsory as in the school sector, has long been regarded by the management and staff of colleges as highly desirable and, partly for that reason, has expanded considerably in recent years. This growth has occurred both among universities and colleges of higher education offering courses leading to Certificates and Post-Graduate Certificates in Education (PGCE), and especially in further education centres offering City and Guilds (C&G) Further Education Teacher's Certificates. As we pointed out in Chapter 1, the National Council for Vocational Qualifications (NCVQ) has taken the attitude that teachers of further education courses which lead to the award of National Vocational Qualifications (NVQs) based on the demonstration of 'competencies' should themselves undertake 'competence-based' training courses. As a result, C&G training courses, and to an extent university courses, are increasingly adopting a competence-based model. This trend is likely to accelerate as, at the end of 1994, the Employment Department (ED) and the Department for Education (DFE) made it clear that they wished to see the development of higher-level, competence-based, NVQs for teachers in further education, and that the delineation of the skills required of lecturers would be a major task for the further education lead body when it came into existence.

Meanwhile, the present provision of initial teacher training for further education falls into two major categories, pre-service and in-service. The former denotes programmes for students who undertake a course of teacher training prior to taking up posts in further education colleges. The students commonly enter a one-year full-time course which leads to a Post-Graduate Certificate in Education (PGCE) directly after completing a first degree programme. The majority are in their early twenties, though there is a significant proportion of mature students with previous industrial or business experience. In the past, these courses were concentrated in five specialist centres: institutions which are now the Bolton Institute of Higher Education, the University of Greenwich (formerly Garnett College, London), the University of Huddersfield, the University of Wolverhampton and the University of Wales, College of Cardiff. These institutions still provide the bulk of these courses, but they have since been joined by others, including, for example: the University of Keele, which has recently introduced a one-year full-time PGCE course in conjunction with Bilston College of Technology in Staffordshire; the University of London Institute of Education, which in 1993 introduced a one-year full-time PGCE in Post-Compulsory Education designed for graduates wishing to teach in further education or sixth-form colleges and based in a partnership with local colleges; Edge Hill College of Higher Education, an affiliated College of the University of Lancaster; and Gwent College of Higher Education, an associate college of the University of Wales.

In terms of student numbers, more numerous are in-service courses, provided on a part-time basis for teachers already working in institutions in the further education sector, though these courses also cater for many who are working in the health service, in adult education, in business, in the services and elsewhere. For example, the University of Greenwich, which in 1989 incorporated Garnett College into what was then Thames Polytechnic, offers what it claims is the largest provision of courses and consultancy in post-compulsory education and training in the UK, catering for over 1000 teachers and lecturers. Its courses include part-time certificates and Post-Graduate Certificates in Education, in Further Education, the Health Professions, Higher Education, Post-Compulsory Education and Training, and Adult Education. As has already been indicated, there has been a growing trend for these and other higher education institutions to collaborate with further education colleges in offering both pre-service and in-service courses. For example, the University of Wolverhampton offers a joint programme with Telford College of Arts and Technology in Shropshire leading to In-service Certificates and Post-Graduate Certificates in Education, and the North East Wales Institute of Higher Education (NEWI) offers a similar programme with Telford College, Shrewsbury College of Arts and Technology, and North Shropshire College. Indeed, many of the 'new' universities, the former polytechnics, have franchised their

Certificate of Education courses to further education colleges so that they can concentrate on degree courses. A typical example of the latter is the BA (Hons) in Education offered by the University of Portsmouth, for which one of the criteria for entry is the possession of a Certificate of Education or its equivalent.

With the conferring of university status upon the former polytechnics, the great bulk of teacher training for further education came into the university sector. As a consequence, the Universities Council for the Education of Teachers (UCET), which promotes and protects the universities' interests in teacher training, hitherto almost entirely in the school sector, has established a new committee for the training of teachers of the post-16 age group, which of course includes those in further education. In addition, the 'new' universities involved in further education teacher training have become concerned that a new lead body for further education might be foisted upon them with little or no consultation. Accordingly, they have established a consortium for post-compulsory education and training, the Universities' Professional Development Consortium (UPDC). All the member universities of UPDC possess business schools which have already set up management verification consortia to verify awards at NVQ Levels 4 and 5, in order to prevent the NCVQ, with what they regard as an undue emphasis on competence-based criteria, doing it for them. The intention is that the UPDC will do the same for NVQs in education and training.

In addition to courses provided by universities and colleges of higher education, another major route to teacher training is provided by the C&G through its Further Education Teacher's Certificate schemes, Course No. 730, which does not of itself lead to a professional qualification conferring qualified teacher status. However, many of the certificate courses described above grant exemption from parts of their courses to holders of 730. Originally, the course was devised for part-time teachers, extending over two years. However, it has been increasingly taken up by full-time teachers, who regard it as a basic or induction course. The numbers attending it have grown steadily in recent years and totalled 10,000 in 1993–94. Of the students attending 730 courses nationally, up to half do not work in further education, coming instead from private training organizations, from the health and caring services, from fire and ambulance services, from the armed forces and elsewhere. In the past few years variants of 730 have been introduced by C&G. Thus, in 1990 730–5 was launched, a 'competency-based' pilot scheme involving 44 centres, very largely further education colleges. Then in 1993, in order to match the requirements of NVQs and the Training and Development Lead Body (TDLB), 730–6 was introduced, in which the 'pilot competencies' were amended. Meanwhile, the traditional course, now entitled 730–7, has continued to run and will be available at least until 1995. C&G's original intention was to phase it out in favour of the competency-based courses, a policy which was in line with that of the government, as laid down by the NCVQ, to establish a framework of NVQs based on national standards for training and development. Indeed, as the 730–6 was compatible with the requirements needed to obtain NVQs at Level 4 in training and development appropriate to the further education sector, C&G submitted it both to the TDLB and the NCVQ for this award. This led to it being accredited at the end of 1994. However, some centres offering 730 have expressed concern about these developments, being less than happy with the move towards competency-based courses, and as a consequence C&G has decided to continue to make the existing 730–7 course available as long as demand for it continues. It is clear, therefore, that in recent years there has been a gradual shift to the use of a 'competency-based' model for teacher training courses in further education, a move which applies both to Certificate of Education and C&G 730 courses. Certainly in the case of the latter, a major reason for this move is that government policy has pushed them in this direction, though they have also been embraced as providing a more valuable and appropriate form of training for certain categories of staff. A few years ago, the TDLB produced its own national standards and criteria for 'role competencies' for trainers and instructors and published its findings according to a rubric laid down by the ED. These were confirmed by work undertaken by the Further Education Unit (FEU), which indicated that they could be adapted for use by the further education colleges,[1] and the general move in this direction has followed. More recently, the TDLB, following criticisms of its standards and qualifications structure, including the not unimportant fact that although further education is a major provider of training and development, it was not included in its original functional analysis, undertook a fundamental review and issued its revisions in the summer of 1994. As a result of many complaints that its dicta were couched in ambiguous and obscure language, it has also attempted to make them more 'user-friendly'. Meanwhile, in broad terms, the C&G programme specifies what are called 'key competencies' or tasks which are to be performed by teachers and also the levels of performance required to achieve each of these tasks. The course itself is typically divided into units and elements of competencies with associated 'performance criteria and range statements', thus adopting the new jargon of the NCVQ. The students are assessed mainly by means of evidence in the form of a 'portfolio' which they gather together, consisting of 'evidence specification' for each unit which they study.

The assessment of the candidates follows a complex procedure involving internal assessors and verifiers and awarding bodies external verifiers, whose roles and qualifications are spelled out in some detail by the awarding body. Thus, the initial assessment of the students is carried out by assessors who, as teachers on the courses, plan with and agree with the students their evidence to be presented to demonstrate their competencies. These are then verified by what are now known as internal verifiers, also members of the college, the term 'verifier' having replaced 'moderator'. Finally, the awarding body appoints external verifiers who ensure that the internal verifiers' assessments are in order and that all the necessary paperwork has been correctly carried out. In order to help ensure that NCVQ standards of quality control are achieved, C&G is moving towards the position where all the above assessors and verifiers are accredited by means of obtaining training and development awards, known cryptically as D32 or D33 for assessors, D34 for internal verifiers and D35 for external verifiers. Indeed, the NCVQ is now moving towards a system requiring all external assessors and verifiers to have such qualifications. Students undertaking C&G 730-6 courses, having covered the ground required to qualify as assessors and verifiers, will have obtained these qualifications without further study. These awards are also available from the Institute of Training and Development, which developed them in the first place, from the Business and Technology Education Council (BTEC), and from the Royal Society of Arts (RSA). However, just possessing them does not necessarily make for a highly qualified assessor or verifier as, in the opinion of at least one critic,[2] they essentially require lecturers to demonstrate only a very small aspect of their work. Moreover, the assessment specifications have been couched in dense and at times impenetrable language which makes them difficult for both lecturers and students to follow. However, just as the TDLB standards on which they are based have recently been revised and made more 'user-friendly', so C&G has revised its assessor and verifier units to make them more comprehensible and to ensure greater consistency in assessment between centres and different awarding bodies. Meanwhile, it is certainly worth pointing out that many institutions offering teacher-training courses have for many years incorporated into their courses many of the features of competence-based curricula without going the whole hog or adopting the term in their titles. Indeed, it could be argued that the traditional 730–7 falls into this category, and, when C&G commissioned an independent review of the scheme, the report concluded that it was in general competence-based. However, its assessment procedures do not quite fit into the format required of a competence-based course, nor is it acceptable for the award of NVQs. For these reasons, C&G has devised the alternatives described above.

Inevitably, the introduction of competence-based courses has resulted in a great deal of argument about their merits and demerits. Indeed, some of those who support them strongly in principle have reservations about how they are operating in practice.[4] The nub of these reservations is that competence-based courses are too inflexible, concentrate on narrow competencies and, most importantly, do not incorporate the philosophical and reflective thinking which underlies and vitalizes good practice. As one critic put it, the interpretation of competence as 'output capability' is too narrow and ignores deeper thinking, feeling, and understanding.[5] Another criticism of the new courses is that they are excessively bureaucratic, involving far too much paperwork, and are too often couched in language that is difficult to understand. However, as we have seen, C&G has responded to this last criticism, by revising their requirements to make them more comprehensible.

In trying to arrive at a considered judgement about competence-based courses, perhaps the key question is 'Have they improved performance in the classroom?' While it is too early, and indeed it may never be possible, to arrive at a definitive answer, there seems to be a general feeling among students undertaking the courses that they will lead both to higher standards in the courses themselves and also eventually to better classroom teaching.[6] Certainly, the portfolios are welcomed as being very valuable and providing good motivation to students, and the range of units which is available is less prescriptive than the old courses and can be tailored better to individual needs. As a result, students are managing their own learning to a greater extent, which in turn helps them to manage the learning of their students in the classroom. Last but not least, as the criteria and procedures are more clearly spelled out than was formerly the case, students know better what is expected of them. Nevertheless, there is no doubt that the introduction of these new courses, based on 'training' principles laid down by the TDLB and followed by the NCVQ, has raised many concerns among those responsible for teaching them, not least because they doubt whether it is possible to develop a single set of learning outcomes for the award of NVQs, as further education has to meet the needs of many different students as well as a range of social and economic needs which embody different cultures and value systems.[7] Moreover, there has not yet appeared a systematic evaluation of how teachers are faring following competence-based training, nor a definitive assessment of its merits and demerits.[8]

Common, however, to many of the courses described above, whether competence-based or not, are some critical issues. In some ways the most important, which affects all of them, is to design course contents which meet the needs of the students who are teaching, or going to teach, in the further education sector. In our view, these should include: some consideration of the major recent developments determining the character of further education; an understanding of how institutions are changing in response to these developments; an appreciation of the problems of resourcing them adequately; a knowledge of the particular needs of adult students; and some acquaintance with the detailed workings and content of core skills, NVQs, credit-based systems and the like. It goes without saying that the needs of pre-service and in-service students are different and must be differently catered for. Teacher trainees should also be introduced to the principles of flexible learning and of student-centred approaches, and should understand the need for the careful monitoring of those they will teach and of the need to keep meticulous records. They should familiarize themselves with the learning resource centres, now introduced by two-thirds of the further education colleges, in which students are relatively free to pursue their own learning with the aid of computers. Last but not least, they should be able to make use of information technology in their teaching; at present, however, it is clear that many staff make little or no use of computer-based learning materials either in their own courses or as a means of facilitating course review and development.[9]

Many further education teacher training courses nowadays make considerable use of 'mentors'. In the case of pre-service courses these are members of college staff responsible for the oversight of students on teaching practice, and for in-service courses they are colleagues of teachers in the colleges undertaking the courses to whom the latter can turn for help and advice. In both cases, they usually play an important part in the assessment of students. In general, these arrangements work well, not least because they establish forms of partnership between the training institutions and the colleges which are valued highly on both sides.[10] However, mentoring is not without its problems, including inevitable disparities in the quality of oversight and help provided by individual mentors and the fact that the process, if it is done properly, is time-consuming and in the great majority of colleges time is at a premium. Another perennial and seemingly insoluble problem faced by some training institutions is their inability to supply courses in the methodology of teaching specific subjects, given the wide range of subject areas their students will be teaching in the colleges. There is a danger, therefore, that further education teachers may be inadequately prepared as teachers of specialisms. To help overcome this problem the training institutions frequently turn to mentors in the colleges, some of whom have difficulties either because they are not properly qualified or because of shortage of time. The demands on mentors in pre-service courses are particularly severe, as they are required to help recent graduates with little or no previous experience of teaching or of further education. In order to prepare mentors for this difficult task, some training institutions are providing 'mentor training' programmes. Finally, mentors can, if anything, become too friendly with those in their charge and as a result are not sufficiently dispassionate when judging their performance. Whatever its shortcomings, mentoring has become widely accepted as desirable by both the institutions and the mentors as having considerable benefits for both teachers and students.

Finally, one group of staff in the further education colleges who perhaps receive less attention than they should are the instructors and technicians. Working for the most part in workshops, such as those concerned with the maintenance of motor vehicles or with electrical, electronic and mechanical engineering, they are often called upon to take responsibility for the assessment of trainees to NVQ standards. In order to do so, they need to acquire at least the D32 Award described above. However, a number of them who wish to progress to obtaining a lecturer appointment and to improve their career prospects enrol on C&G 730 courses and, in some cases, go further and complete a Certificate in Education course.

Although C&G is the main provider of teacher-training courses for staff in further education, some of the other awarding bodies, notably the RSA, also make a signficant contribution. The RSA offers a wide range of qualifications for teachers and trainers including the Teachers' Certificate in Office Studies and a Diploma in Teaching and Learning in Adult Basic Education. Of increasing importance are its courses leading to Diplomas in the Teaching of English as a Second Language and Teaching of English as a Foreign Language, as the demand for these courses by would-be teachers has grown considerably in recent years. Like C&G, the RSA also offer awards, based on TDLB standards, for assessors and verifiers. Another awarding body active in this field is the Pitman Examinations Institute, which offers a range of NCVQ-accredited awards in the examination and assessment of employment skills, including, for example, accounting and retailing, the latter being awarded in association with C&G.

Over the years since the Haycocks Report on the initial training of further education appeared in the later 1970s,[11] a number of training institutions has put together a coherent system of further education teacher training along the lines proposed in the reports. An example is the programme offered by the College of Cardiff of the University of Wales, which falls into three stages: the first is an induction course of 40 hours instruction which leads to a Stage I Certificate in Education (Further Education); the second takes up 130 hours, including at least 24 hours of practical teaching, and leads to a Stage II Certificate, equivalent to C&G 730-7 Further and Adult Education Teachers' Certificate; and the third leads to the PGCE or to the Certificate in Education (Further Education).[12] Just how well integrated and coherent post-Haycock programmes of this kind are, it is difficult to say. In some cases, Stage III is not always sufficiently well distinguished from the earlier stages, nor has its proper purpose always been well thought out.

Finally, it is worth noting that while the training of further education teachers in England and Wales has been going through an uncertain period, with indecision and dilatoriness about the establishment and future role of a further education lead body and concern about the introduction of competence-based criteria, the situation in Scotland is very different. There, the links between quality and further education teacher training have been clearly identified,[13] and steps have been taken to ensure that a standard course is provided by an institution of higher education.

Staff Development in Further Education

As the term denotes, staff development is concerned with the professional and personal development of the staff of the further education sector, whether they are engaged in teaching, administration, or other duties. As we have made clear many times in this book, the enormous changes which have taken place in further education during recent years have made these duties more complex and onerous and have greatly increased the need to provide programmes of staff development and to ensure that staff have the opportunity to attend them. The changes in employment conditions which have been taking place in the past year or so are themselves a response to the need for colleges to show greater flexibility in the courses they offer and when and how they teach them, to improve the quality of their programmes and to cater for growing numbers of students. For the individual teachers and lecturers, the demands made upon them can be divided into four main categories.[14] Firstly, they will have to offer a wide range of teaching methodologies, from traditional teaching through seminar and tutorial work to individual counselling. Secondly, as the structure of courses becomes more complex, with modularization and similar developments, and as the need to liaise with employers, validating bodies, the college management and others becomes more pressing, so course management becomes more time-consuming and demanding. Thirdly, more and more lecturers will become involved in tutoring and acting as mentors for students and colleagues undertaking courses of teacher training. Lastly, there is an increasing need to update teaching materials and teaching methods, particularly those involving the use of information technology, as at present too many teaching and support staff lack information technology skills. Moreover, increasing numbers of staff will need to be redeployed from their traditional teaching and administrative duties into other areas of work, and for this purpose will need proper retraining.

In the late 1970s, there was a considerable increase in the provision of staff development in the colleges, many of whom appointed staff development officers to promote and coordinate the work. Much of it was financed by earmarked government funding which came to an end with the passing of the 1992 Further and Higher Education Act, and there were fears that, following the incorporation of the colleges, there would be a steep decline in provision. In practice, this does not seem to have happened and most colleges still have staff development officers and make reasonable provision, partly because of the demand from the funding councils and the Training and Enterprise Councils (TECs) that the colleges pay regard to the quality of their courses. However, provision seems uneven and some college managements place more emphasis on the value of staff development than others.[15] The amount of money spent on staff development is a matter for the colleges themselves to determine. A recent survey carried out in London by the National Association of Teachers in Further and Higher Education (NATFHE) showed that colleges devoted to it varying sums, ranging from 1 to 4 per cent of their staff budget. The categories of staff development underwritten by the colleges also vary with management development, the acquisition of assessor and verifier qualifications, appraisal and GNVQs and NVQs featuring high on the list.[16]

The changing role of further reducation staff requires a coherent system of staff development which can and should take a variety of forms. At the level of the institutions themselves, many colleges provide 'in-house' programmes of workshops and conferences through which they buy in expertise, often from higher education institutions. When, before incorporation, staff development programmes were financed by the local authorities, they concentrated very largely on the teaching staff of the colleges. Nowadays, there has sensibly been a move towards a 'whole staff' approach in which non-teaching staff are also included in the provision of staff development. However, what the colleges can offer is severely circumscribed by the limited funds available to them, and although some colleges make substantial arrangements for staff development, others are finding it hard to make even modest provision. At the regional level, as we have seen, the successors to the regional advisory councils (RACs), in response to needs identified by the colleges, offer a range of training programmes, including those for staff wishing to become accredited as NVQ verifiers and assessors and for those teaching GNVQ courses. Throughout the country, the higher education teacher-training institutions are increasingly involved in providing programmes of staff development. These vary from offering the services of their staff to individual colleges for the provision of custom-built programmes, to higher degree programmes. The latter have grown considerably in number as more and more teachers, in further education as in the schools, see the acquisition of a master's degree, especially one in educational management, as a prerequisite for obtaining a senior management post.[17] Indeed, no fewer than 49 universities and four colleges of higher education in England alone now offer masters' degree courses in educational management, the great majority on a part-time basis. While most students attending them are working in schools, a significant proportion comes from the further education sector. Many of the courses are provided on a modular basis and often include adult and post-compulsory education as one of the areas on offer. Many of the universities and colleges offering these courses take into account previous experience gained by teachers, and a variety of schemes is in use, including accreditation of prior learning (APL), accreditation of prior and experiential learning (APEL) and credit accumulation and transfer (CAT). A likely future development is the offering of taught doctoral courses on a similar basis and, indeed, the University of Bristol has recently introduced a PhD programme, based on weekend attendance, consisting of core studies, a range of options, and a dissertation.

Staff development programmes are also provided by the examining and validating bodies, a good example being the GNVQ workshops and training sessions provided by C&G in conjunction with the RACs. In the last few years, there has been a considerable expansion of entrepreneurial activities in the field of staff development, consisting mainly of the running of conferences of one kind or another, some sponsored by private organizations and some by the colleges themselves. A national body which was established in 1977 to represent staff with special interests in the field is the National Association for Staff Development (NASD). It has members in a wide range of further education establishments, holds twice-yearly conferences around the country, and issues a publication *NASD Journal*, which appears twice a year. As we have indicated in Chapter 2, both the FEU and the Further Education Staff College (FESC), which merged to form the Further Education Development Association (FEDA) in April 1995, have played important roles in promoting and sustaining staff development. Finally, a valuable source of information on current developments in this field, as in others of relevance to further education, is *EDUCA*, the Digest for Vocational Education and Training.

Research into Further Education

One of the ways in which programmes of staff development have been instituted and refined is through research into further education, though the range of its concerns extends well beyond that, of course. Indeed, research into those areas with which the further education sector is concerned is very broad-ranging and is undertaken by many people in many agencies. As it overlaps, for example, both with major areas of the educational system and with training for industry and business and is also as strongly influenced by social research and public policy review, it is necessary to take a wide view.[18] On that basis, research of relevance to further education is undertaken by government ministries, notably the ED and the DFE; by the TECs; by agencies such as the FEU, the FESC, the National Foundation for Educational Research (NFER) and the NCVQ; by bodies such as C&G; by the universities and colleges of higher education; by the further education colleges themselves; by organizations such as the Further Education Research Association and the Association for Colleges (AfC); by private consultancies; and by the European Community. And even this list is not exhaustive. However, the total volume of research into areas with which further education is concerned is still relatively small by comparison with the school sector or higher education. It is heartening, therefore, that the Economic and Social Science Research Council (ESRC) has recently funded a major research project, entitled 'The Learning Society', much of which bears directly on the work of the further eduction colleges.

The ED plays a particularly large part in commissioning and financing research into vocational education and training, outstripping the DFE in this respect, though occasionally they do jointly commission research as, for example, a survey of the use of the National Record of Vocational Achievement (NROVA) by employers, training organizations and college staff. Although the ED generally concentrates on evaluations of government-funded programmes such as training credits, Investors in People (IIP) and the operation of the TECs, its activities spread much more widely. For example, projects completed in 1993 and 1994 and their results published include international comparisons of vocational education and training by the University of Leicester, the implementation of NVQs and their Scottish equivalents by employers, by the Institute of Manpower Studies of the University of Sussex, and individuals' decision-making about lifetime learning, by a private consulting company.[19] In addition to its *Annual Report on Research*, it issues useful publications in the form of *ED Research News*, which lists, among other things, newly commissioned research projects, and *Research Briefs*, which are short, clear summaries of longer research reports. As one of the problems with research in these areas is that the results are frequently poorly disseminated,[20] these publications are particularly welcome. One reason for the relatively poor dissemination of research findings into further education is the paucity of journals devoted to the subject. Two of the very few in this area are the *Journal of Further and Higher Education* and the *Vocational Aspect of Education*. The latter is holding its first conference, on Developments and Research in Vocational Education and Training, in the summer of 1995. Finally, the TECs, who derive the greater part of their funds from the ED, also undertake some research projects, usually on a relatively small scale, of local interest and importance. For example, the Greater Peterborough TEC has, jointly with a Cambridge University examining board, initiated a scheme to measure the success of local schools and colleges in preparing their students for careers.

As we have commented earlier in the book, the FEU and the FESC, which have a long and honourable record of undertaking research into patterns of key interest to further education, were in April 1995 brought together to form FEDA, under its chief executive, Stephen Crowne, formerly head of the qualifications division in the further education branch of the DFE. As we have indicated, while the FEU concentrated mainly on curricular matters, including, for example, issues relating to GNVQ and modularization, it also commissioned research on a wide range of topics relevant to the sector such as guidance and learner support services and equal opportunities. The FESC, on the other hand, focused on the organization and managerial aspects of further education institutions. Just how effective FEDA will be in continuing the work of its two predecessors remains to be seen, though it is significant that its remit will include the staff development of further education teachers. At the time of writing, it is appointing two directors, one for training and consultancy in England and in Wales, and the other for research and information. As one would expect, research undertaken by the NCVQ has been mainly concerned with the introduction and working out of NVQs and GNVQs, while the NFER, though mainly concerned with the school sector, has from time to time undertaken specific research programmes in further education. Among the validating bodies, C&G has a research unit which in 1993, for example, prepared staff support materials, including an NVQ assessment handbook, and also evaluated the introduction of GNVQs into a sample of its centres. It also participated in ED projects to set parameters for computer-aided assessment for both NVQs and GNVQs.

Among the higher education institutions, a number of universities have established research centres concerned with various aspects of vocational education and training, including Manchester University's Centre for Education and Employment Research, under its director Professor Alan Smithers, and the University of Warwick's Centre for Education and Industry. Both of these centres have been very active in the field, publishing books and reports to which reference has been made elsewhere in the book. Warwick has also held a number of influential conferences on such topics as education and training policy in the USA and the UK and, with the aid of ED funding, which has now dried up, set up a forum, or network of researchers, concerned with vocational education and training and, in particular, public policy towards it. More recently, the University of Keele has established a Centre for Social Research in Education. Under its director, Professor Denis Gleeson, it is currently investigating the attitude of young people towards work-related training. Another university-based research activity funded by the ED, which reported in the summer of 1994, was the GNVQ Assessment Review Project, conducted by staff of the University of London Institute of Education.[21] As we have observed, its report argued that fundamental changes to GNVQ assessment are required if it is to be sustainable in the large numbers of centres offering the programme, and the awarding bodies have already introduced a number of chages which will help to meet some of its criticisms.

While it has always been part of the business of universities to undertake research, this has not been the case with further education colleges. However, they are increasingly becoming involved as, since becoming 'independent' of their local authorities, some of them are looking to research studies to help them increase funding, improve teaching quality and promote staff development, not to mention raising the status of their institutions.[22] As a consequence, there has been a considerable upsurge of interest in research in the colleges and an expansion in activity. Most college-based research studies are, as one would expect, concerned with applied rather than pure research, as, for example, an ED-funded project at Salisbury College, which examined ways in which flexible learning can help small businesses to give staff training.[23] Other topics include the investigation of the amount of participation in further education in given localities, the reason for excessive wastage on courses, and the ways in which retention and success rates can be improved. One of the factors which has promoted applied research has been the need to respond to requests for information of one kind or another from the funding councils. Where further education colleges have a substantial proportion of their students concerned with programmes of higher education, as in the case of North East Surrey College of Technology, for example, then they tend to place more emphasis on research, partly because it provides opportunities for attracting funding and, more important perhaps, because it infuses and verifies teaching at this level.[22] The growth in higher education in the further education colleges in recent years has led the Society for Research into Higher Education (SRHE) to establish in 1994 a further education/higher education network, whose aims are to focus on research activities in the interface between the two sectors and to consider issues such as models of collaboration and the impact of curriculum change, including the development of GNVQs. However, funding for research is limited and there is much competition for it, not least from private training agencies and private consultancies, who inevitably siphon away some of the funds that would otherwise be available to the publicly maintained colleges. Within the further education institutions, as elsewhere, the term 'research' can be used in different ways, including the sharing and development of good practice by individuals involving relatively small amounts of time. Just such an approach is recommended in the field of adult education, where research and its dissemination constitute relatively uncharted territory.[24]

Among the teachers' organizations concerned with the promotion and dissemination of research into further education is the Further Education Research Association (FERA). Established in 1973, it draws its members very largely from staff in further education colleges. It publishes a useful source of up-to-date information on current research into further education in the form of the *FERA Bulletin* and holds two conferences annually on such subjects as Developing Research Cultures in Further Education and Initial Diagnostic Assessment, which were discussed at its May 1993 and 1994 conferences respectively.[25] FERA's main concern is to enable staff of member institutions to come together to discuss individual research projects as well as to undertake collaborative research. To assist this process it has planned to share information about current activities by means of a research database. The Association for Colleges (AfC) has also been active in promoting research by funding projects in colleges. The primary aim of this research is to help develop the further education curriculum by using new ideas of flexible learning and modern learning technology to increase participation and attainment and improve learning productivity. To these ends, it has funded a dozen fellowship schemes in colleges in the UK, including one college in Wales and a consortium of colleges in Northern Ireland, by means of three-year grants, financed by the Esme Fairbairn Foundation.

Finally, the European Commission has also been active in promoting and financing research into vocational education and training. At the beginning of 1994, it issued a document outlining its priorities for research programmes during the period 1994–98, which included the development and dissemination of innovations in education and training systems, the identification of new generic processes linking education and training to the changes affecting science and technology, and the evaluation of the implications of European integration in order to identify the European Community's contribution to improving education and training systems in Europe. Across such a wide remit, groups and individuals active in further education research in England and Wales undoubedly have much to contribute, though obtaining funds from the European Community to finance research in these areas is undoubtedly a complex and bureaucratic business. Meanwhile, an agency of the European Community very active in disseminating information on vocational and educational training across its member states is the European Centre for the Development of Vocational Training, which is located in Thessaloniki. Among its many publications is a series of reports on the procedures of each of the member states for certifying vocational qualifications and it is currently putting together a directory of teacher training across the European Community which will include information on vocational training and the provision of training through educational bodies, vocational training and company organizations.

From the foregoing account of research into vocational education and training it is clear that there is a great deal of activity, probably more than ever before. Much of it has been stimulated by the major changes that have been taking place in the further education sector, together with such factors as the requirement by the funding councils for the colleges to provide them with information, and the opportunity which incorporation has given to the colleges to finance their own research studies. Clearly, the range of research activity is vast and its quality very variable. Indeed, precise definition of what constitutes research into further education is difficult, if not impossible, to provide and some of which passes for research undoubtedly has a relatively weak empirical base and is small-scale and local. Moreover, once completed, the dissemination of research findings frequently leaves a great deal to be desired. Nevertheless, research into further education has much to contribute to the successful development of the sector and one of the heartening features in recent years has been its expansion within some of the colleges themselves. This development could be encouraged and fostered in a variety of ways, including: the provision of information within the colleges about sources of funding; the sharing of information with other researchers working in similar fields; support from the college management for research activity, including making time available for staff for this purpose; and, last but not least, the introduction of an element of rigour into these activites, including, where possible, the publication of results.[26]

Notes and References

1   Further Education Unit, *TDLB Standards in Further Education*, London, FEU, February 1992; for a critique of this paper, see A. Chown, 'TDLB Standards in FE', *Journal of Further and Higher Education*, **16** (3), 52–59 (1992).

2   S. Besley, 'Becoming an accredited assessor and verifier', *EDUCA*, **138**, 10–11 (1993).

3   P. Garland, 'Competence based qualifications for FE lecturers', *Journal of Further and Higher Education*, **17** (2), 86–89 (1993).

4   A. Chown and J. Last, 'Can the NCVQ model be used for teacher training?' *Journal of Further and Higher Education*, **17**(2), 15–26 (1993).

5   F. Foden, *The Education of Part-time Teachers in Further and Adult Education*, University of Leeds, Leeds, 1992, pp. 215–216.

6   S. Stark, 'Competence based teacher training programme in FE', *Journal of Further and Higher Education*, **16** (1), 86–89 (1992); and S. Stark and G. McAleary, 'Initiating a competence based teacher training programme', *Journal of Further and Higher Education*, **16** (2), 87–90 (1992).

7   A. Chown and J. Last, 'Can the NCVQ model be used for teacher training?' *Journal of Further and Higher Education*, **17** (2), 145–126 (1993), citing S. Otter, *Learning Outcomes in Higher Education*, UDACE, 1992.

8   K. Eccleston, 'Mastering the job', *Education*, 30 July 1993, p. 89.

9   D. Adcock, 'Equipping staff for the job', *Times Higher Educational Supplement*, 10 June 1994, p. vi.

10 I. Abbott and L. Evans, 'Finding time for mentoring', *Times Higher Educational Supplement*, 15 June 1994.

11 Advisory Committee on the Supply and Training of Teachers, Further Education Sub-Committee, *The Training of Teachers for Further Education* (First Haycocks Report), London, DES, 1975; and *The Training of Adult Education and Part-time Further Education Teachers* London, DES (Second

Haycocks Report), 1978. These Reports culminated in the issuing by the Advisory Committee on the Supply and Education of Teachers of *A Coherent System of Initial Teacher Training for Serving FE Teachers*, London, DES, 1983.

12 J. Richards, 'The in-service training of further education teachers in Wales', *The Welsh Journal of Education*, **3** (2), 10–13 (1994). For a recent and full account of further education teacher training in England and Wales, see M. Young, N. Lucas and G. Sharp, *Teacher Education for the Further Education Sector: Training the Lecturer of the Future*, London, University of London Institute of Education, October 1994.

13 Scottish Office Education Department, *The Initial Training of Further Education College Lecturers* (Anderson Report), Edinburgh, SOED, August 1993.

14 L. McBean, 'Try a little sensitivity', *Times Educational Supplement*, College Management, 3 June 1994, p. 6.

15 P. Martinez, 'Staff development in the FE sector', *NASD Journal*, **31**, 3–9 (1994).

16 Ibid., p. 7.

17 I. Lawrence, 'Master plans', *Times Educational Supplement*, 18 November 1994, p. 1.

18 Ibid.

19 Employment Department, *ED Research News*, October 1994, p. 3.

20 J. Twining, 'Waste of money?' *EDUCA*, **130** (1993).

21 'GNVQ assessment in practice', *EDUCA*, **145**, 11 (1994).

22 T. Tysome, 'Climbing ladders to cash and kudos', *Times Higher Educational Supplement*, 16 September 1993.

23 S. Dear and G. Hall, 'Profiting out of personal contact', *Times Educational Supplement*, College Management, 23 September 1994, p. 9.

24 M. Howells, 'Ripe for the picking', *Education*, 2 September 1994, p. 174.

25 C. Ward, 'Initial diagnostic assessment', *EDUCA*, **143**, 12 (1994) and *FERA Bulletin*, **58** (1994).

26 Taken from the summary of the conclusions of a Further Education Research Association Conference on 'Developing Research Cultures in FE', May 1993, reported in *EDUCA*, **134**, 14 (1993).

Seven

Further Education in Wales

In a previous book on this subject, we observed that in the early 1980s the responsibility for all non-university institutions of higher and further education in the principality became that of the Secretary of State for Wales, with administrative responsibility having been transferred from the Department of Education and Science (DES), as it then was, to the Welsh Office,[1] though of course the ultimate responsibility for the provision of education in Wales, as in England, rests with Parliament. Within the Welsh Office in Cardiff, there is an education department which has a further and higher education division with overall responsibility for the planning and development of the two sectors. In a relatively small country like Wales, it is reasonable to bring both higher and further education under one roof, an arrangement which is also reflected, as we have seen, in the fact that there is a common chief executive for both the higher and further education funding councils, though they are separate bodies with separate chairmen. Also housed in the Welsh Office is the Welsh Training, Enterprise and Education Directorate (TEED) of the Employment Department (ED).

In all, the further education sector in Wales comprises 27 further education, sixth-form and tertiary colleges which were formerly LEA-maintained and became independent corporations on 1 April 1993. These include three self-standing colleges of agriculture and horticulture, at Llysfasi in North Wales; the Welsh College of Horticulture, also in North Wales; and Pencoed in South Wales. In addition, four general further education colleges have units offering land-based studies. Five other institutions – a denominational sixth-form college; Coleg Harlech, an adult residential college; two Workers' Educational Association Districts; and the YMCA (Wales) – joined the sector by designation. As can be seen in Figure 7.1, a number of colleges now operate on several sites, including Coleg Powys and the two tertiary colleges, in Gwynedd and Gwent. The Further Education Funding Council for Wales (FEFCW) also funds further education provision in six higher education colleges and in LEA and other sponsored institutions. Table 7.1 shows that the further education sector in Wales catered for just over 137,000 students in the session 1993–94. Of these, almost 75,000 were in

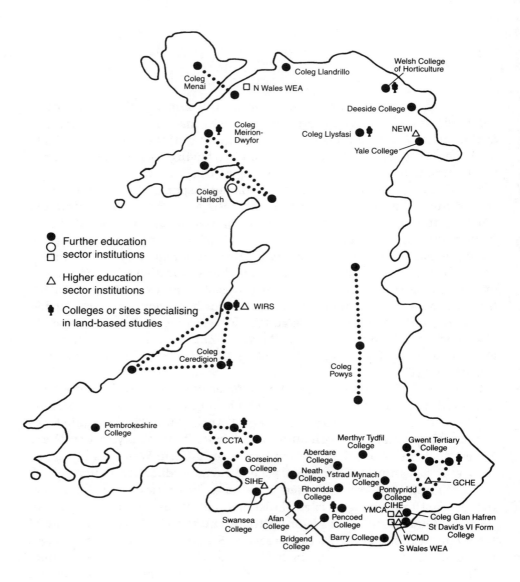

Figure 7.1: *Further education establishments in Wales* (Reproduced by permission of the Further Education Funding Council for Wales)

Table 7.1. Student enrolments in Further Education in Wales, 1993–94

A.   **By mode of attendance**

Full-time and sandwich		35,569
Part-time day and block release		15,056
Not released		28,535
Other		57,893
	Total	137,053

B.   **By types of colleges**

General further education colleges		74,723
Tertiary colleges		20,194
Sixth-form colleges		4,741
Colleges of agriculture and horticulture		2,172
Other institutions		35,223
	Total	137,053

Source: FEFCW Bulletin, 94/7 'Further Education Early Students Enrolments, 1993–94', August 1994.[2]

general further education colleges, over 20,000 in the two Welsh tertiary colleges, over 4700 in the sixth-form colleges, 2172 in the principality's three colleges of agriculture or horticulture, and over 35,000 in other institutions, the great majority being students enrolled on further education courses in the Cardiff Institute of Higher Education, the North East Wales Institute of Higher Education, the Welsh College of Music and Drama in Cardiff, and the Swansea Institute of Higher Education. During the past four or five years, the biggest rise has been in full-time students, whose numbers increased by about 50 per cent between 1988–89 and 1992–93. By comparison, students enrolled on day- and block-release programmes declined from just over 20,000 to just under 16,000 over the same period. The Welsh colleges have been given a target of a 9.7 per cent yearly increase in student numbers, which is higher than the English target of 8 per cent. Although there has been an overall increase in student enrolment in the session 1993–94 of the order of 5 per cent,[2] it falls well short of this target.

As in England, the administration and funding of further education has changed substantially since the provisions of the 1992 Further and Higher Education Act came into force. Perhaps the key body in this respect is the FEFCW, or Cyngor Cyllido Addysg Bellach Cymru (CCABC), which, as we have observed earlier, operates in a broadly similar fashion to its English equivalent. Under its chairman, Malcolm Wallace, an industrialist, its aims and objectives are also very similar, though they do include the maintenance and development of opportunities for bilingual provision and Welsh language education, and the support and promotion of activities and initiatives which contribute to the educational, social, economic, cultural and linguistic well-being of the people of Wales. The fact that the chief executive of the FEFCW, Professor John Andrews, holds the same position on the Higher Education Funding Council for Wales has advantages in that it helps to allow proper account to be taken of the not inconsiderable degree of overlap between the two sectors, as for example in the case of the substantial numbers of students in the Welsh institutes and colleges of higher education who are undertaking further education courses funded by the FEFCW.

The FEFCW has established a quality assessment committee which has formulated an assessment framework which provides for reports both on individual institutions, which are issued at least once every four years, and also on the quality of provision by 'programme areas' across the sector. To date, a number of major programme areas, including business studies, engineering, and construction have been reviewed. However, unlike the Further Education Funding Council for England (FEFC), the FEFCW does not have its own inspectorate, relying instead on the school inspectorate in the shape of the office of Her Majesty's Chief Inspector (OHMCI) which acts as the FEFCW's agent. Working alongside the assessors from OHMCI are associate assessors drawn from staff working in further education institutions, and the FEFCW has stated that over the next few years it wants to move from an inspectorial approach to one in which the institutions' own evaluations play a central part in the assessment procedures.[3] In addition to its chairman and chief executive, the FEFCW has 11 members drawn largely from industry and the further education institutions in Wales. There are two observers on the FEFCW, one being Sir William Stubbs, the chief executive of the FEFC, and the other an assistant secretary at the Welsh Office. Unlike the membership of the Higher Education Funding Council for Wales, there is no Scottish representative, presumably because compared to the universities in the two countries, their further education sectors differ more substantially from one another. Though the FEFCW is therefore broadly representative of vocational education and training interests in Wales, it is nevertheless one of the many quangos which control considerable swathes of Welsh affairs, their numbers having more than doubled in the past 15 years. This development has been particularly criticized in Wales on the grounds that they are non-elected bodies which have been brought into being by a Conservative government, whose party holds only six of the 38 Welsh parliamentary seats.[4]

Certainly, the FEFCW, like many of the other Welsh quangos, distributes very substantial sums of public money, the recurrent funding allocation for 1994–95, for example, amounting to £137 million. As in England, it has adopted a funding framework consisting of three major elements, based on the recruitment, learning and attainment stages of education. For the session 1994–95, it based its funding distribution on a modified methodology designed to encourage colleges to increase their provision of vocational courses, especially for day-release students whose numbers, as we have seen, have declined in recent years, and for adults returning to college to improve existing skills or obtain new ones.[5] Included in the new funding formula are elements which encourage colleges to improve their marketing of courses, to provide more guidance and counselling for students, especially for those from socially and economically deprived areas and sparsely populated rural regions, and to assist with the extra costs of rural colleges and those providing bilingual courses. The FEFCW has also expressed considerable concern at what it terms the 'generally poor condition and inadequate capacity of the further education estate in Wales,[6] and provided capital funds of £20 million for 1994–95 to help improve the situation. As in the case of England, a proportion of the funds in the hands of the Training and Enterprise Councils (TECs) in Wales for work-related further education has been transferred to the FEFCW, and is being allocated to institutions by the recurrent funding methodology currently in use.

Within the principality, there are seven TECs broadly performing the same functions as their counterparts in England. However, there are some differences: for example, at least two of them, the West Wales TEC based on Swansea, and TARGED, the North West Wales TEC, based on Bangor, have policies strongly supporting bilingualism. This is hardly surprising given that the areas they serve contain populations with large numbers of Welsh speakers: in the case of the West Wales TEC area, 29 per cent speak Welsh, and in the case of TARGED, the figure is about 60 per cent. The West Wales TEC, which has the largest economically employed population in Wales, also contains a small but significant proportion of people from ethnic minorities, including Bangladeshis, Chinese, Indians, Pakistanis and Iranians, and developing their skills is an important part of its responsibilities. As in England, the Welsh TECs have come together to form a national body, known as the Council of TECs in Wales, with an office in Newtown in Powys. The council meets regularly and undertakes research and prepares reports. It is currently working on issues relating to work-related further education.

In the summer of 1994, its chairman, John Troth, who is chairman of the North East Wales TEC, complained publicly that the TECs' prime objective of raising skill levels and achieving the national education and training targets was being hampered by bureaucracy imposed upon them by the Welsh office, which was so preoccupied with financial problems afflicting the Welsh development agencies that it was neglecting support for the TECs.[7] Finally, the Welsh TECs are represented on the TECs National Council based in London, and John Troth is currently chairman of the National Council's Training Policy Group.

Until the passing of the 1992 Further and Higher Education Act, the

Welsh LEAs and the Welsh Joint Education Committee (WJEC) played important roles in the administration and delivery of further education in the principality. However, in Wales, as in England, the LEAs now play only a rudimentary part in further education. Thus the WJEC, which was unique in being both the regional advisory council (RAC) for further education and the major examining body of Wales, has lost its responsibility for further education and become a body primarily concerned with the school sector. Partly in order to fill the vacuum left by the virtual departure of the LEAs and the WJEC from the further education scene, the Welsh further education colleges came together to set up FFORWM (The Welsh Colleges Forum), a private limited company launched in July 1993. Prior to that, it functioned as an informal association of colleges. It includes in its membership the sixth-form colleges and colleges of agriculture and horticulture, and its principal aims are to foster collaboration and cooperation between colleges, to initiate staff and curriculum development programmes, to organize centrally services and facilities as required by the colleges, to act as a focal point for discussion, and to represent the sector as required and to raise its profile both in the UK and abroad. It was initially supported by a grant from the FEFCW to help it undertake its management, staff and curriculum function, but this support came to an end in March 1995, and FFORWM is now expected to be self-supporting and, in this respect, like the East Anglian RAC, it becomes owned by the colleges. In the relatively short time since its creation, it has held a regular programme of staff development conferences, workshops and seminars and has undertaken a number of curriculum initiatives, especially the Wales Modularization and Credit-Based Development Project. The last-named is a pilot project, funded by TEED, which FFORWM took over from the WJEC, and its purpose is to develop a system of modularization which will be accepted by all the Welsh further education colleges. FFORWM also has close links with the further education colleges in England through the Association for Colleges (AfC) and, indeed, all colleges enjoy joint membership of both bodies on payment of a single consolidated fee.

Finally, given the part it plays in fostering staff development and curriculum initiatives, FFORWM is naturally concerned that the amalgamation of the Further Education Unit (FEU) and the Further Education Staff College (FESC) into one body, the Further Education Development Agency (FEDA), should take into account Welsh circumstances. On the one hand, it wants FEDA to provide more than a token of support to Wales, and on the other it wishes, rightly, to ensure that duplication is minimized.[8] From recent developments, including the nomination of two members of the FEFCW and two from FFORWM's board of directors to the board of FEDA, the appointment of a director for training and consultancy, whose remit includes Wales as well as England, and the existence of an FEU regional development officer for Wales, whose future involvement has been guaranteed by the Welsh Office, it seems that attention will indeed be paid to Welsh interests.

Across the further education sector as a whole in Wales a number of developments are taking place, some of which are particular to the principality and some of which it has in common with England. One area of debate, which we have already mentioned in passing, is that of bilingualism, which in this context means the ability to speak both Welsh and English. The 1991 census[9] showed that 17.35 per cent of the adult population spoke Welsh, but this is a figure which is progressively growing. Major factors contributing to this process are the growth in Welsh-medium schools and the inclusion of Welsh in the National Curriculum as a core foundation subject in all other schools, and the impact of the Welsh Language Act 1993 and its statutory Welsh Language Board, with the resultant demand for Welsh-speaking staff within private and public sector organizations. This latter development is reflected in the publication of the FEFCW's annual reports and bulletins, as well as Welsh Office publications such as *The Charter for Further Education* and *Further and Higher Education and Training Statistics in Wales* as bilingual publications.

Another major body involved in promoting Welsh language education in both schools and colleges has been, and is, the WJEC. This it sees as one of its signficant continuing responsibilities[10] and in the late 1980s it established a development project, with financial support from the then Training Agency (TA) of the ED, entitled 'The Development of Bilingualism in work-related Further Education'. This project was set up following a 1984 report by Her Majesty's Inspectors (HMI) which described bilingual provision in the further education sector as piecemeal and uncoordinated, depending to a large extent on the enthusiasm of individuals. The WJEC report confirmed that command of the Welsh language was considered as a key skill for people working in a range of occupations, both in essentially Welsh-speaking areas and also, to some extent, in more Anglicized areas. As a number of colleges took part in the project to develop bilingual provision, so it became established in the mainstream of many of them, taking various forms, including dedicated bilingual courses, optional Welsh medium/bilingual units in Business and Technology Education Council (BTEC) national courses, and Welsh/bilingual assignments in English-medium courses. Since then, General National Vocational Qualifications (GNVQs) have been introduced into colleges and schools in Wales and the National Council for Vocational Qualifications (NCVQ) has fully accepted the need for them to be available through the medium of Welsh. However, if they are to be widely available, there will be a concomitant need for Welsh language assessors, and, as specific training will be required to ensure sufficient numbers are qualified, arrangements are being made by the Welsh

TECs to this end. Interestingly, the situation concerning National Vocational Qualifications (NVQs) has been slightly different. As possession of an NVQ is a statement to the effect that the individual is competent to perform at work to clearly defined standards throughout the UK, initially all students seeking to gain NVQs through the medium of Welsh were required to demonstrate competence in English as well as Welsh. However, following a change in NCVQ policies it is now possible to gain an NVQ entirely through the medium of Welsh.

Another body concerned with bilingualism was the Welsh Language Education Development Committee (WLEDC), Pwyllgor Datblygu Addysg Gymraeg, known as PDAG for short, which was established by the WJEC in the mid-1980s at the behest of the Secretary of State for Wales and was funded by the Welsh Office. It was given the remit of maintaining a strategic overview of Welsh language education and, in respect of further education, drew upon the expertise of the WJEC Bilingual Further Education Panel. However, in 1993, following the transfer of responsibility for funding the local and national coordination of Welsh language classes for adults to the FEFCW, the WLEDC was disbanded at the very time when, according to one observer, 'it had forged effective relations with many agencies and reached a degree of maturity in fulfilling its responsibilities.'[10] However, in 1994, the FEFCW, in partnership with the Higher Education Funding Council for Wales, established a joint review group to consider the provision of Welsh language education for adults. Its report,[9] which appeared in May 1994, recommended that institutions and other organizations should join together to establish consortia providing courses for adults through the medium of Welsh, and that the FEFCW should fund all sub-higher Welsh for adults provision through its new recurrent funding mechanism. These recommendations have been accepted by the FEFCW, which has agreed both to support up to 12 consortia and to increase funding for this purpose.

Furthermore, recognizing the importance of utilizing the WJEC's unique experience in coordinating and developing Welsh language education for adults, the FEFCW came rapidly to an agreement with it whereby it procured the services of a Welsh for adults officer, whose remit included establishing local consortia, disseminating good practice in the provision of Welsh for adults, and providing the executive of the FEFCW with advice on strategic developments. Subsequently, the FEFCW has taken steps to increase Welsh-medium further education provision for other groups of students by modifying its funding mechanism. To this end it is commissioning a study on the resource materials required for NVQ teaching and learning through the medium of Welsh. It has also adopted a collaborative approach with the Welsh Office, FFORWM, the Curriculum and Assessment Authority for Wales, or Awdurdod Cwricwlwm ac Asesu

Cymru (ACAC), the examining and validating bodies (EVBs) and the Welsh Language Board (WLB), normally referred to as Y Bwrdd Iaith. The latter body, a quango arising from the 1992 Welsh Language Act, has recently published guidelines on the steps to be taken by all public bodies to ensure parity in the use of Welsh and English. It has also appointed a person with very substantial experience of pioneering bilingual developments in schools and colleges as a senior education officer with responsibility for the post-16 age group.

FFORWM and the FEU have also taken steps to foster such developments, the former by establishing a bilingual working party and the latter by commissioning research into how best to provide Welsh-medium GNVQ assessments. There are, however, some issues which need to be considered when preparing Welsh-only assessment procedures. Some colleges, for example, are advocating bilingual assessment procedures: it is important to define more specifically the methodology of delivery, and there is a great need for appropriate and comprehensive staff development programmes. For these reasons, there is a great deal to be said for reinstating the further education lecturers' bilingual forum, Fforwm Darlithwyr Bellach Ddwyieithog, which contributed greatly to developments in this field in the period up to April 1993.

Finally, an interesting Welsh language development is being sponsored by Menter a Busnes, a Welsh-medium business and management education centre established with the support of the Development Board for Rural Wales and the Welsh Development Agency to 'promote the enterprise of Welsh speakers'. To this end, one of its current projects is to enable colleges throughout Wales to offer business and management courses in Welsh and multicultural courses. In this context, Menter a Busnes, in conjunction with TARGED, has produced a number of Welsh language texts on business and management, for example *Ewrop Heddiw* (Europe Today), for use in courses leading to GNVQ Levels 2 and 3. While these are desirable developments, catering for Welsh-speaking students poses problems, among them finding suitable placements in business and industry in which to acquire work experience.

One area in which the Welsh further education colleges seem to be taking the lead is in the development of credit accumulation and transfer (CAT) schemes on a systematic basis. As we have seen, FFORWM is currently developing a system of unitization and modularization which is supported by all the colleges in the principality. An integral part of that project is the working out with the Open College Networks in Wales of accreditation processes. However, the movement towards a credit accumulation and transfer (CAT) system, by which students can accumulate credits on the successful completion of part of a qualification and are able to change or build on this achievement if they wish to take a different course, has been accelerating in Wales for several years. Some of the groundwork of such a national scheme was carried out by a joint Welsh Office–TEED-funded modularization project run by the WJEC which started in 1991 with seven colleges, entitled 'Towards a Flexible FE System in Wales'.[11] The first phase focused on modular developments within specific curricular areas and the second, in 1992–93, included additional work on cross-curricular processes and the establishment of a college network. The final report[12] stressed the vital importance of establishing a common currency for modules in order to enable the exchange of students between colleges to take place. Undoubtedly, the WJEC project helped both to increase the awareness of the need for flexibility to increase participation in Welsh further education and also to persuade the Welsh Office and TEED to finance a successor project managed by FFORWM, to which we have referred earlier in this chapter. The aims of this project include helping to develop a CAT system which has currency across the whole of the UK, since it is based on the FEU's specification for a common credit framework, with units and credit for learner achievement awarded by Open College Networks. To this end, the Welsh Office has made it clear that it would like to see a 'unitized' curriculum operating for 80 per cent of Welsh further education courses by September 1996. In the meantime, increasing numbers of Welsh colleges have contributed to the growth of a centrally coordinated credit framework which is flexible enough to allow individual colleges to adapt the curricula they offer. The movement towards credit accumulation has been further strengthened by the introduction in September 1994 of the FEFCW's new funding methodology to which we have referred. While considerable progress has clearly been made, the establishment of a national CAT system still has some hurdles to clear. One is to develop arrangements that allow transfer across the further education–higher education interface and which apply to higher education institutions in the principality, including the University of Wales. Another is to ensure that the Welsh modular system is comparable with that in England. Discussions are currently taking place to bring into being an effective interchange between English and Welsh users of a CAT framework encompassing national qualifications. Indeed, if the FEFCW's new funding methodology, which links funding to a qualifications credit scheme, turns out to be as sophisticated as its proponents believe, it might well be followed by the further education sector in England.[13]

In Wales, as in England, one effect of the financial stringencies presently afflicting colleges is to lead some of them to seek mergers. The first Welsh example since incorporation is Coleg Menai, which came into existence on 1 August 1994 following the amalgamation of Gwynedd Technical College in Bangor and Coleg Pencraig, based at Llangefni, in Anglesey. The merger was supported both by the FEFCW, which believed that it would bring about a rationalization of courses and resources and an improved service to students, and also by the Welsh Office.[14] This example in North Wales might well be followed by others in the principality in the next few years: for example, at the time of writing, the Colleges at Pontypridd and Rhondda have, with the approval of the FEFCW, submitted plans for their merger to the Secretary of State for Wales, and are awaiting his decision. Meanwhile, the creation of another 'merged' institution, in North Wales Coleg Meirion–Dwyfor, has not been without its problems. The first tertiary and the first bilingual college in that part of the country, it opened in September 1993 and it operates on several sites, with its main campus at Dolgellau. Its creation led to the secondary schools within its thinly populated, rural catchment area shedding their sixth forms, so that they now cater only for the 11 to 16 age range. The consequence is that many students who formerly attended nearby sixth forms now have to travel considerable distances to the college. Understandably, many parents have objected to this state of affairs and, indeed, the secondary school in Bala is threatening to opt out of local authority control unless its sixth form is reinstated. The local authority, Gwynedd, has agreed that the Welsh Office should decide the issue and its verdict is awaited. This example highlights the problem of creating a tertiary college in a rural area where inevitably many students will have to travel considerable distances in order to attend courses.

As far as teacher training for further education in Wales is concerned, we have already made a number of references to it in the previous chapter. The University of Wales College of Cardiff, which pioneered initial teacher training for further education, remains a major centre, offering a range of both full-time and part-time courses and also validating courses offered in other institutions.[15] Other Welsh higher education institutions heavily engaged in further education teacher training are the Cardiff Institute, Gwent College and the North East Wales Institute of Higher Education. The Cardiff Institute of Higher Education offers both a Postgraduate Certificate in Education (PGCE) and a Certificate in Education (Further Education) for teachers in higher, further and adult education, leisure and youth workers, and training personnel in the forces, industry or business. Gwent College of Higher Education, at Newport, in addition to offering courses leading to PGCEs, BA Hons, and MAs, all in education and training, franchises Dyfed LEA to teach PGCE and Certificate of Education (Further Education) courses on its behalf. The North East Wales Institute of Higher Education is also active in this field. Until fairly recently, its courses were run under the auspices of the University of Wales College of Cardiff; now, however, it is directly accountable to the University of Wales Validation Unit. It offers both PGCE and Certificate in Education (Further Education) courses and in 1993 introduced a competence-based scheme leading to these qualifications. It also has a series of franchising arrangements which we noted in the previous chapter, whereby Stage III 'Haycocks-style' programmes leading to PGCE and Certificate in Education (Further Education) qualifications are available at further education colleges at Oswestry, Shrewsbury and Telford, in Shropshire. Finally, in conjunction with the University College of North Wales in Bangor, it offers a part-time modular course, taught at weekends, leading either to a Master of Education or a Diploma in Education.

As far as the provision of staff development in Welsh colleges is concerned, as we have seen FFORWM is playing an active part. In the relatively short time since its inception, it has devised a programme covering five key functional areas: estate management, marketing, management information systems, personnel, and strategic planning. Its aim is to help colleges raise the level of performance in the sector and, to this end, is currently running a series of seminars and conferences. As in England, the proportion of their resources devoted to staff development varies from college to college.

Two areas in which developments in Wales lag behind those in England are in the achievement of the national education and training targets and in the numbers of women who secure equal access to education and training to that of men. In the first instance, Wales is behind the rest of the UK, and while progress is being made, further improvement is necessary. For example, while the Foundation Target 1 is that 80 per cent of young people should reach NVQ Level 2 or its equivalent by 1997, in 1993 the percentage in Wales was 57.9 compared to 61.5 in the UK as a whole, while for Foundation Target 3, by which 50 per cent of young people should reach NVQ Level 3 by 2000, the comparable figures were 30.6 per cent and 36.9 per cent. The same is broadly true of the national targets relating to Investors in People (IIP).[16] Secondly, according to a report published by the Equal Opportunities Commission (EOC),[17] while more and more women in Wales are enrolling on courses of education and training – for the first time, nearly equal numbers of men and women are signing up – they are still less likely to achieve recognized qualifications than women in other parts of the UK. Moreover, they choose to study much more traditional subjects than women elsewhere in the country and lag behind in vocational qualifications. The EOC report is of interest for another reason, namely that it is one of the few examples of research conducted by the EOC to concentrate solely on Wales. Indeed, it is unfortunately the case that research into matters of importance and interest to further education is even less substantial in Wales than it is in England. Indeed, relatively little has been written about further education in Wales at all, other than HMI reports, WJEC documents and a small number of Masters' dissertations. However, with the establishment of the FEFCW and FFORWM, the situation is improving.

As in England, the European dimension of further education provision in Wales is of increasing importance. This is recognized by the Welsh TECs, who claim that, in the community of the European Union, they are in a position to respond quickly to opportunities to pilot European-funded programmes and to test new European initiatives.[18] To this end, the seven Welsh TECs, who have raised millions of pounds from European Community funds for Welsh-based projects, support a full-time post at the Wales European Centre in Brussels, while the Welsh WEA also has a full-time representative. At the local level, the Welsh colleges are increasingly including 'the European dimension' in their courses and expanding the number of exchanges between their students and those in the membership states of the European Community. One such is Swansea College, which in November 1992 was awarded first prize in a national UK competition organized by the Bureau for Educational Exchange for excellence in curriculum development in European studies.

Following the signing of the Maastricht Treaty in 1993 and its much-touted principle of 'subsidiarity', whereby the member states are free, to an extent, of the centralized control of Brussels, it is perhaps paradoxical that in the UK, as we have seen, the control of the central government in Whitehall over the educational system in England and in Wales has grown considerably in the last few years. This development is particularly objectionable to many in Wales, who point out that the Conservative government had relatively little popular support at the last general election and that undue centralization is alien to Welsh traditions of power-sharing and local democracy. Indeed, all three opposition parties in Wales foresee the need for an elected Welsh Assembly with its own legislative and tax-raising powers,[19] which could therefore come into existence in the not too distant future. If this should happen, an almost inevitable consequence is that the further education sector, in common with schools and higher education, would become accountable to it, instead of at present having to respond to the diktat of the Welsh Office and the FEFCW. Whether the latter would survive is open to question but, if so, its membership is likely to be more democratically arrived at. For the transfer of major powers from the Welsh Office to a Welsh Assembly to be fully effective, its advocates rightly contend that the specific arrangements for the funding and administration of the whole educational system in Wales, from pre-school to higher education, need to be the subject of a major debate.[20]

As we have seen, the further education sector in Wales, as in England, is very complex and, partly because of its vocational function, is subject to continual and often rapid change. Unlike further education in Scotland, it is also predominantly dependent on non-indigenous examining and validating bodies. Moreover, historically, it has been much less valued than the higher education sector and there has been too little public awareness of its important contribution to the economic well-being of the principality. However, there has been some improvement in this regard in recent years: for example, as a result of representation by FFORWM, the AfC's publication *FE Now!* includes a regular feature on developments in further education in Wales. Nevertheless, further steps need to be taken both to increase coverage in the media of the work of the further education institutions and also to promote a full debate on how best to provide a sound basis for making decisions about the future of the sector. Over the last five or ten years it has served the principality well: participation has increased considerably and a number of important initiatives have been taken, including growth in bilingual provision – fuelled in part because, in the words of an authoritative commentator on the Welsh educational scene, 'Parents, including large numbers of monoglot English, now rightly perceive the ability to speak and write Welsh as an economic and social asset'[21] – and the working towards a national system of modular courses and credit accumulation. Clearly, the further education sector has a crucial role to play in the education and training of the workforce in the principality.

Notes and References

1   L. M. Cantor and I. F. Roberts, *Further Education Today: A Critical Review*, London, Routledge & Kegan Paul, 1986 (3rd edn), p. 152.
2   'Further Education Early Students Enrolment, 1993/94', *FEFCW Bulletin* Cardiff, FEFCW *94/7*, 22 (1994).
3   Further Education Funding Council for Wales, *Annual Review, 1992–93*, Cardiff, FEFCW, **19**.
4   T. Heath, 'Placemen take control of Quangoland', *Guardian*, 19 November 1993.
5   T. Tysome, 'FE funding aims at the mature', *Times Higher Educational Supplement*, 6 May 1994, p. 4.
6   Further Education Funding Council for Wales, *Annual Review, 1992–93*, Cardiff, FEFCW, **19**, 13.
7   T. Tysome, 'Welsh training heads fire Redwood warning rocket', *Times Higher Educational Supplement*, 12 August 1994.
8   'The Review of the FEU and the Staff College', Letter dated 28 September 1993 from the Chief Executive of FFORWM to the Chief Executive of the Welsh Funding Councils.
9   Further Education Funding Council for Wales/Higher Education Funding Council for Wales, *Report of the Welsh for Adults Joint Review Group*, Cardiff, FEFCW, Table 3, May 1994.
10 C. Heycock, 'Week by week', *Education*, 8 April 1994, p. 268.
11 N. Merrick, 'Welsh colleges join the rush', *Times Educational Supplement*, 2 July 1993, p. 7.
12 Welsh Joint Education Committee, *Towards a Flexible Further Education System in Wales*, Phase II, Cardiff, September, 1992–June 1993.
13 T. Tysome, 'Welsh funders back cash for college credit scheme', *Times Higher Education Supplement*, 28 Janaury 1994.

14 M. Prestage, 'Competition ends with a new name', *Times Educational Supplement*, 28 October 1994, p. 8.

15 J. Richards, 'The in-service training of further education teachers in Wales', *Welsh Journal of Education*, **3** (2), 10–13 (1994).

16 Information supplied by the Welsh Office in a letter dated 1 December 1994.

17 Equal Opportunities Commission, *Equality Through Education*, London, EOC, 1994.

18 Welsh Training and Enterprise Councils, *Impact of TEC in Wales*, Treforest, Pontypridd, Mid-Glamorgan TEC, 1995.

19 I. Bowen Rees, 'The restoration of local democracy in Wales', *Transactions of the Honourable Society of Cymmrodorion*, 1993, pp. 139–181.

20 P. Jeremy, 'Keep Major in the Marches', *Times Educational Supplement*, 9 May 1993.

21 G. Elwyn Jones, 'Bordering on the new Renaissance', *Times Educational Supplement*, 30 September 1994.

Eight

The Future of Further Education

The present state of further education is rapidly changing. There have been many occasions in this book where we have had to use a cautious 'at the time of writing ...' or 'this is under review'. Under the circumstances it may seem foolhardy to add a chapter about the future. There are some issues, however, which we consider it worth indicating as being of likely future interest. The purpose of this chapter is to reflect upon the main themes of the preceding ones, to consider how they might develop in the next few years, and, as appropriate, to make our own suggestions about where further education might be going.

Government Responsibility

The frustration felt by many of those working in the education and training systems as a result of the division of responsibility between the Employment Department (ED) and the Department for Education (DFE) has been expressed frequently through calls for a merger between the two.[1] This proposal has not proved attractive to the present government, since the areas of clearly separate responsibility, for instance the National Curriculum for the DFE, or Jobcentres for the ED, are as important as the areas of overlap. One might surmise that it is equally convenient for both departments to have fire drawn away from policies to organizational matters. After several years of tension between them, the succession of interchange of posts between senior civil servants from the two departments followed in 1994 by the move to the DFE as secretary of state by Gillian Shephard, formerly Secretary of State for Employment, has ensured a reasonable level of understanding. It might be supposed that the 'ownership' of the Further Education Funding Council for England (FEFC) by DFE, managing the institutions, is balanced by the 'ownership' of the National Council for Vocational Qualifications (NCVQ) by the ED, managing the qualification structure. However, as direct responsibility for these shifts from government ministers to quangos like the funding councils, the question of whether or not there should be one overriding ministerial responsibility for education and training becomes less pertinent.

Quangos and Democracy

In theory, the government has handed over many of its responsibilities to the 'quangos' (quasi-autonomous non-governmental organizations).[2] As far as further education is concerned, there has been a shift away from local government to centralized control, and a change in the structure of the organizations with which the system has to deal. For the most part, colleges have lost their links with their local councils and education authorities. Some local councillors have managed to retain positions on college governing bodies as personal nominees, representative of the community, but they are becoming increasingly rare. A few local education authorities (LEAs) still provide advisory services under contract to their former further education colleges, but within a newly defined 'purchaser–client' relationship, which gives the college the choice of whether to continue to purchase these services. Colleges now have a wide range of sources of advice, as evidenced by the number of private consultants and consultancy firms bidding for business with them. Possible changes in the structure of local government will therefore have little direct impact on the colleges and may even increase the choice of services which can be bought.

With the shift of control has come a loss of accountability through democratic representation, especially at a local level. In the past, any question about the operation of a college by the curious and the dissatisfied could be raised through their local council. This may not always have proved effective, but at least the line of communication was clear. To raise the same query now would involve a direct approach to the management of the college, possibly followed by contact with a member of the governing body, who will certainly not have a representative relationship with the enquirer, and so is unlikely to have the same sense of obligation to provide a response. The relevant funding council may be prepared to take an interest if the question is one which affects general policy, or on matters of probity related to the college as a whole[3] but, beyond that, an aggrieved person has a direct line to the Secretary of State, backed up by the system of judicial review. In practical terms, the smooth running of a college is firmly in the hands of the principal and senior staff. While in higher education there are occasional examples of staff members being removed from the corporations (the governing bodies of the universities), further education colleges have generally, even if in some cases reluctantly, kept their teaching and non-teaching staff representatives. They and the teacher unions appear to have appointed themselves guardians of institutional probity, and the National Associations of Teachers in Further and Higher Education (NATFHE), for example, has instituted what it calls a 'whistle blowers' hotline', whereby lecturers who are concerned with falling standards, or possibly suspect corrupt practices, but are reluctant to raise the issues in their own colleges for fear of being disciplined, may communicate their concerns to the union for possible subsequent action. As a matter of principle, the increased emphasis on customer relations has meant that managers take complaints very seriously, not primarily as a matter of democratic necessity, but because it is good business. What the effect of this will eventually be on educational decision-making remains to be seen. Matters of educational policy cannot always be decided by market forces, since there are issues of natural justice and social equity at stake. The government has become very sensitive about criticism of the quangos and is likely to act with more responsibility and discretion when appointing members in the future.

The funding councils rapidly adopted a positive stance towards provision for students with special educational needs, and have provided sufficiently generous funding for them to guarantee a future place for them in further education. This policy has effectively countered what would have undoubtedly been the effects of a purely market-driven planning mechanism in colleges, and indeed almost all further education colleges now make some provision for students with special needs. The full review of the Tomlinson committee will be published after this book goes to press, but the funding councils are expected to continue support of special education arrangements, which have a prominent place in their remit.

Another example of where a local authority might have planned local provision, but often failed to do so, is in decisions about mergers between institutions. Here, the funding councils are in no stronger a position within current government policy than a local authority might have been. They are considering issuing guidelines on the subject and might encourage the merger of a small college of art with either a further or higher education neighbour, and have done so on a number of occasions. They might also endorse a merger between a sixth-form college and a further education college, but are in practice likely to wait for the proposal to come after one of the parties, probably a small sixth-form college, decides that it can no longer sustain itself financially. If, however, several local schools decide to establish or expand their sixth forms, or a well-established grant-maintained school decides to alter its composition, the colleges affected, and the funding councils, can only comment on the proposals.[4] During the autumn of 1994, a group of college principals from the Further Education Campaign Group, supported by Sir Christopher Ball in his role as chairman of the National Advisory Council for Careers and Educational Guidance, attempted to express their alarm about this matter. To an extent, this concern was echoed in the joint FEFC/OFSTED report on 16–19 Guidance in schools and colleges.[5] The waste of resources in the post-16 sector, already unearthed by the Audit Commission, may eventually be traced partly to the under-achievement of the secondary sector, and the often misleading advice given to young people in the interests of boosting school rolls. Standards of probity will need to be demonstrated uniformly across the educational world.

Whether there are significant changes to the situation described above will depend to a considerable extent upon whether there is a change of government at the next general election. While both the main opposition parties are avowing a return to more democratic control of publicly funded institutions,[6] there are reasons why they might find it more convenient to leave matters largely as they are. Firstly, there are some major questions about the effectiveness of local government systems which demand sophisticated management but depend upon councillors who are volunteers. Local government positions have gradually become less attractive to would-be local politicians as the influence of local government has been eroded, and a new government might prefer to exert its influence by changing the government nominations on the boards of quangos, rather than going through the prolonged and uncertain procedures needed to get local government bodies on its side. As long as the funding councils stay free of major fraud, a new government might be happy to allow them to continue. Planned measures such as the avoidance of too many small sixth forms can be equally effectively implemented directly from the centre by the funding councils, which might also suit a government of any hue.

Research and Development in Further Education

One area in which further education colleges benefit from a proliferation of funding bodies is in research and development. It has not been unknown in the past for two government departments to fund development projects on broadly the same area within one institution, although they are now more aware of the dangers of waste through duplication. Nevertheless, colleges which have an interest in innovation can often substantially increase their income from exploiting the variety of government funding sources. Up to now, such developments have been on a relatively small scale, with a short time-span for completion. A typical Further Education Unit (FEU)-funded project, for instance, would rarely exceed £20,000 for a year or two's work. EC projects might appear to have been more generously funded, but would probably include an element for student support. We have now started to see an increasing interest in research into and about further education, which despite its importance is undoubtedly the least well-researched education sector in the country. As we noted in Chapter 6, the Association for Colleges (AfC) obtained some useful research funds from the Esmee Fairbairn Trust, and in 1995 the Economic and Social Science Research Council (ESRC) will begin a £4 million programme, entitled 'The Learning Society', which among other things is designed to increase research activity in further education colleges, mainly in partnership with institutions of higher education. Those further education colleges with substantial programes of higher education will not remain satisfied with their allocations from the research councils, and they have already shown themselves adept at obtaining funding from commercial sources. As far as research into further education is concerned, many colleges have now established development units with well-qualified staff who, if the research councils were to modify their stance on funding matters, are quite capable of giving higher education researchers a run for their money.

The next battle in further education may well not be between competing government policy departments, but between the quangos themselves, that is between the further and higher education funding councils. There is now sufficient overlap between further and higher education to justify a review of the funding of higher education in further education colleges, as well as the flow of research funds. The higher education sector has somewhat embarrassed the government by hitting its student expansion targets two years early, and parts of it have failed to demonstrate a significant reduction in costs. Problems of financing students undertaking programmes of higher education mean that there is likely to be greater difficulty in funding mature students or those from poorer families, especially if their education involves a move away from home. Rather than incur a huge debt, such students may well prefer to obtain a higher education qualification part-time, or full-time at an institution near to their home. Consequently, instead of establishing even more universities, the present or next government is likely to look for ways of adjusting the balance of expenditure away from the present higher education institutions. Farnborough College, for example, is already on record as claiming to provide a degree course for around £700 per student per year, as against the average cost in higher education institutions of nearer to £4000. It should be said, however, that some further education colleges seek to offer higher education courses, even if they run at a loss, for the perceived prestige they bring. Nevertheless, if further education colleges can offer relatively cheap courses and students are willing to take them, it seems inevitable that there will be a comparative review of expenditure by the funding councils and possibly changes in the present funding systems.

There are similar possibilities for change among the research funding bodies. The FEU and the Further Education Staff College (FESC) are now both within the ambit of the new Further Education Development Agency (FEDA). Such a body is not only in a good position to channel funds into the sector from other government departments, such as the ED and the Department of Trade and Industry (DTI), it is also able to affect the stance of industry and the research councils towards further education. FEDA is, of course, an arm of the Further Education Funding Council for England (FEFC), which makes the latter's position even more monopolistic.

Meanwhile, FEDA has been given a remit to work in Wales, as well as in England, and there is no doubt that Welsh college principals will be as keen as any others to receive funds from it if it begins to channel money to them, on any appreciable scale, for research and development.

Education for Older Adults

The area of provision which does seem to have sustained some damage as a result of the establishment of the funding councils, and the advance of a market-led policy, is adult education of the type still funded by local authorities. Apart from courses of study which carry a vocational qualification, and are therefore funded by the funding councils, there remain many opportunities for adults to study for pleasure only, or to develop skills which have no obvious vocational relevance. Since the establishment of the funding councils, enrolments to these courses have seen some decline, and their fees have risen as local subsidies have been withdrawn. As a consequence there are no institutional arrangements within the colleges themselves for funding recreational courses for any age group other than at full cost, except for those which are subsidized by LEAs. The social costs of this change may be substantial. Many thousands of elderly and isolated people have derived benefit from their local adult education opportunities, and they have not all wished to follow award-bearing courses. These classes have not been the exclusive preserve of the middle class, although such people predominate. In any case, age and isolation are not generally affected by income or social status. Two future effects, therefore, may be increased pressure on social and medical services from people who are denied the therapy of adult education, in a period of early retirement and increased life expectancy, as well as a rapid growth, already in evidence, of privately provided adult education, often expensively in exclusive surroundings. The lecture cruise to historic sites, or the country weekend course on soft furnishing, are typical examples. Elsewhere in Europe, the adult education service as we know it in this country hardly exists. In France, for example, while there are opportunities for adults to learn vocational skills, or to improve their basic education, the recreational aspects of adult education are catered for by voluntary societies of enthusiasts. It may well be that the fragmentation of society in the UK has gone so far that we are incapable of forming such local interest groups on any scale, in which case the loss of the adult education service will do significant further social damage.

There is still considerable scope for development in colleges as far as the vocational education of adults is concerned. Many colleges have expanded their full-time provision for younger people to a participation level in excess of 80 per cent of school leavers. This leaves them with only one major target for future expansion, which is the group left out of educational opportunities twenty years ago, namely the over-40s. They are among the least well educated and most likely to be long-term unemployed. With twenty years of working life ahead, an investment in their education and training is worthwhile, if colleges can adapt themselves to their needs. Most of the parts of the jigsaw which, once in place, will respond to these needs already exist; however, many colleges have yet to assemble them. The accreditation of prior learning will give recognition to existing experience and avoid too much time-wasting; National Vocational Qualifications (NVQs) offer a flexible framework for the accreditation of achievements in the workplace or in college; college resource centres and roll-on, roll-off enrolments allow study at a time and place relevant to the adult learner; information technology allows access to work skills and information banks which were never predicted when the over-40s received their initial education; and there are ample training opportunities in personal and managerial skills for those able to benefit from them. The major obstacles, as always, remain institutional, financial and attitudinal. If the colleges are to adopt the necessary approach and bring about the right degree of cultural change, then the professional development of the teachers and support staff will need to be as carefully planned as that of the students.[7]

International Comparisons

Many recent developments in post-compulsory education have had their roots in a desire to challenge international competition, and retain and increase the economic well-being of the country. The increase in staying on after the compulsory school-leaving age, the growth in participation in higher education, and the modernization of the qualification structure have all supported the shift away from traditional heavy productive industry to an intelligence-based, commercial and service culture which would be internationally competitive. Towards the end of 1994, there were some indications that the strategy might be working, at least in the short term. Graduate employment is rising, as are the attainments of school leavers as measured by their qualifications. Those most likely to be unemployed are those with few or no qualifications, and the increased participation in higher education seems to be providing a more flexible workforce, as well as taking a large proportion of younger people out of the full-time labour market altogether, as was the government's aim ten years ago. More young people have had the opportunity to work and study abroad, thanks to the various EC programmes which encourage exchanges and awareness-raising visits. Young people have better language skills, and are more internationally minded than a decade ago. Certainly, they face increased competition from well-educated and enterprising young people, most of them with excellent English, from the other countries of the European Union and those soon hoping to join it from the states of central Europe.

Unfortunately for the UK many of our competitors are moving ahead even faster than we are. The targets for educational development elsewhere in the world are more ambitious than in the UK and the levels of investment higher. Two examples will suffice. Firstly, in France the government's aim is to have 80 per cent of the school-leaving population reaching university entrance standard by means of the various forms of the Baccalaureate by the year 2000, while in the UK the national training target figure to an equivalent level is 50 per cent, although there is pressure to adjust it upwards following consultations with the National Advisory Council for Education and Training Targets. Secondly, in South Korea, these participation levels have already been exceeded.[8] Government and private investment in education in the fast-growing economies of the Pacific rim exceeds anything likely to be possible in the relatively slow-moving systems of western Europe.

It may well be that the most responsive training systems will be those based in commercial and industrial concerns, which already finance a greater part of the vocational education and training in this country than is found in the public sector. In order to do this, however, employers will need to build on a base of solid achievement during compulsory schooling, and in the years immediately following. There are some doubts as to whether the existing achievements at A-level, or even in the hardly fledged General National Vocational Qualifications (GNVQs), will provide this base. GNVQs have yet to establish and prove themselves. A-level GCE, however, is widely regarded as the benchmark against which other systems are measured. While its standards are widely applauded, its narrowness is not, and even the Head Masters' Conference is now pressing for a change in the post-16 examination system, to provide the kind of broad-based but demanding academic education that young Germans find in the Abitur, or the French in the Baccalaureate. Most worrying is the fall-off in scientific study at A-level, despite the provision within the National Curriculum for every school leaver to take at least a double science qualification. There are genuine grounds for concern that the basis for future technological innovation is being eroded by a shortage of appropriately educated young people.

The ability of higher education institutions to respond to an intake of lower-achieving students than they are used to could be a critical factor. One reason for the unpopularity of science at A-level has been the knowledge that highly paid scientific jobs are relatively rare. What may be needed, therefore, is a small elite of highly able scientists and a larger corps of well-education technicians. As long as the new generation of graduates understands that its job prospects are not necessarily those of a graduate a decade ago, the supply of appropriately educated technical personnel may be secure. A major question is whether that supply can be more appropriately and economically secured in further education colleges, rather than in universities. When making international comparisons, it is very easy to compare the home product with another at a level with which it does not strictly compare.

A Flexible Workforce

If it is true that the future well-being of the nation depends on a ready supply of well-educated, flexible and adaptable people, this must also be true of further education college staff. Some of their jobs are unrecognizable from those to which they were appointed ten or fifteen years ago. On the other hand, many of them remain uncomfortably the same. They are uncomfortable because of the pressure to recognize that change is inevitable conflicts with an equal and understandable pressure to retain features which recognize that teaching is a professional and demanding activity. The changes in college management since the 1992 Act have created a division between managers and teachers. Those teachers with sufficiently senior status to be put on the management salary 'spine' were the first to feel the pinch of new terms and conditions of employment. These terms have gradually reinforced the importance of their managerial activities, and significant increases in the administrative work of colleges have made it more difficult for these staff to sustain their lecturing role. Other colleges have decided that it is more appropriate for administrative work to be done by administrators, and have gradually reduced the number of staff paid as lecturers, and increased the numbers of lower-paid administrators. The supply of well-qualified administrators is such that it has been possible to create hybrid posts, not of lecturers who do administrative work, but of lower-paid administrators who have class contact with students. For example, NATFHE, the lecturers' union, has unearthed an 'academic facilitator', a former lecturer, made redundant, and re-employed on a new contract which gives him the job of recording attainments against NVQ competencies, as demonstrated by students in a workshop. He works 38 hours a week, for 47 weeks a year, for less pay than a lecturer.

This example encapsulates the fears of college lecturers faced with the decision of whether or not to sign the new further education college contracts. Certainly, the future of employee relations in further education will be enacted against a background of less generous funding and working conditions than were common in the past. There will be an increase in pay negotiations conducted by individual colleges with their staff, albeit within a framework agreed by larger groupings of colleges, and in pay settlements with individuals with 'spot' salaries, rather than a stately progression up incremental pay scales. There will be performance-related pay for a larger proportion of the teaching force. There will be a much greater proportion of the work done by part-time staff, and where these staff have specialist expertise they will demand payment outside a 'normal' pay range. The concept of tying pay to academic levels of work, which is already seriously eroded, may well disappear altogether. The role of the teacher unions in further education has remained surprisingly protective, in comparison with those in other industries. NATFHE, for example, fought a very successful battle against the wholesale implementation of new contracts by the Colleges' Employers' Forum (CEF) during the autumn of 1994. As more staff and more colleges move over to new forms of contract, however, the unions will need to re-think their role although they will retain an important position in the representation of both groups and individuals. As European-style employee councils take effect in British industry, it may well be that the teacher unions can create a new kind of dialogue with college management for the improved running of colleges, for the representation of individuals caught in the industrial relations cross-fire, and for the modification of some of the more lunatic confrontational positions taken during the early stages of incorporation. The completion of the jigsaw of provision for training adults referred to above will be less cumbersome within a more flexible framework of working practices. Colleges whose staff fail to adapt may well find themselves in such serious financial difficulties, compared to others in the sector, that they go under.

These changes in role are bringing with them concerns about the most appropriate form of training for further education lecturers. The universities may well manage to speak sufficiently coherently to defend their concept of teacher education against the pressures from the National Council for Vocational Qualifications (NCVQ)-driven competence movement. To be truly effective, however, they will have to convince the DFE, the funding councils and any future education lead body that they have an important part to play in further education teacher training and much successful experience to offer. Up till now, the DFE and the funding councils seem largely to have ignored or forgotten the existence of and the need for further education teaching training. Meanwhile, there is a fine example of good practice in this field to be found in Scotland and much could be learned from it.[9]

Relationship with Industry

Further education colleges, by comparison with their sixth-form college bedfellows, have grown and thrived on their relationship with industry and commerce. The relationship has not always been stable or amicable, but it has provided an important *raison d'être*. There are aspects of the new further education which put this relationship under threat. Firstly, as we have seen, colleges are not the main providers of workplace training; instead, employers provide the bulk of this themselves. Where further education colleges are not able to provide what employers need, at a level and price they can afford, they will continue to go elsewhere. Secondly, the traditional forms of work-related training are under threat. In 1992–93, for example, attendance on part-time day- and block-release programmes fell by 7 per cent. Although the Training and Enterprise Councils (TECs) may not survive in their current form, they will still exert a significant influence through their spending power and contracting practices. Successful colleges are adapting to new demands, but it is a difficult and not necessarily profitable shift. Thirdly, it is much more difficult under these circumstances for colleges to consult with local employers about the needs for training. The latter will certainly not speak with one voice, and as the scope and range of industry have changed, so the bodies representing employers have changed with them. Moreover, the TECs have not all proved to have an adequate voice. Owners of small businesses are not much given to taking time off work for committee meetings at employers' federations. Fourthly, and for similar reasons, it may become much more difficult to attract employers to serve on college corporations. Those who do have the time, or who regard it as part of their job, typically the personnel and training director of a large local company, may become more and more removed from the real customer base of the college, especially if there has been a major shift to full-time study, or adult learners. The consultation with employers which used to be a required part of all submissions for new courses to the Business and Technology Education Council (BTEC), for instance, may be further supplanted by the impact of lead bodies, devising prescriptions for competence on behalf of the NCVQ at a national level. As employers become more distant from everyday college operations, the chance of persuading them to invest directly in the equipping of a training facility, as they have done in the past, diminishes.

The basis of a new relationship between further education and industry will require a substantial effort of marketing by the colleges, selling their expertise to a new kind of employer who may in turn be responsible to a head office outside the UK which sets its standard of training from its own national system. For example, Far Eastern multinational companies in the UK have very different models of workplace training from those typically found in the UK. Meanwhile, the Confederation of British Industry (CBI) has been reported as refusing to rule out the possibility of supporting a compulsory training levy on employers, a subject which is now back on its agenda.[10] The future may be more like the past, after all.

Despite some entrenched attitudes, the cornerstone of the further education system in England and Wales over the last hundred years has been its ability to adapt to change. Today, colleges are running fast, some in order to stand still, others to carry flags which others are only just catching sight of. There has been a significant growth in learning resource centres, available on demand, and well equipped with new technology, with teaching assistance on standby throughout the day and evening. When a major company like Ford offered its workers the chance to join a class in any subject of their choice, their local college lecturers were in the plant during the night shift, meeting the need. Some colleges may still be slow in answering their telephones during August, but others have adopted a quality standard that answers before the fourth ring, and gives an intelligent and helpful reply to the query after that. It is a standard to which many industrial concerns might still aspire. The critical mass required to support the new demands on colleges may be such that the smaller ones will not survive into the 21st century. If that happens, many smaller communities will lose easy access to further education opportunities unless new, more flexible methods of delivery are developed. This will be quite possible using the new technological developments in communications, provided sufficient investment is made in the future, probably by government sources. Interestingly, the Labour Party has already announced a policy initiative to investigate the costs and feasibility of such a development for education.

Finally, this may be the last opportunity to provide a book of this kind in written form. The next collection of information and ideas on the further education system is very likely to be on some form of electronic record. In any case, many of today's readers will have already searched available sources of information on a handy database, accessible through the Internet or its successor facility. The day of the 'virtual college' will have arrived.

Notes and References

1   At the time of going to press, the effects of the merger of the training responsibilities of the former Employment Department into the new Department of Education and Employment have yet to be worked through.

2   See Charter 88 Trust, *Extra-Governmental Organisations in the United Kingdom and their Accountability*, London, 1994.

3   See, for example, FEFC enquiry into the governance and management of Wilmorton Tertiary College, Derby, Coventry, FEFC, November 1994.

4   'Sixth Sense', *Times Educational Supplement*, 16 September 1994.

5   FEFC/OFSTED, *Guidance*, A Joint Report, Coventry, FEFC, September 1994.

6   For example, in an article in *The Guardian* on 23 May 1994, Michael Meacher, then the Labour shadow public affairs minister, was quoted as saying, 'Where they have usurped powers which should only be exercised by elected authorities – higher and further education, training, health trusts, urban development and regional road networks – Labour will abolish these quangos and restore their functions to elected authorities.'

7   R. Gorringe *et al.*, *Changing the Culture of a College*, Coombe Lodge Report, Blagdon, Further Education Staff College, 1994.

8   OFSTED, *Secondary Education in the Republic of Korea*, London, HMSO,

1994. This report states that over 90 per cent of South Koreans aged 16 to 18 are in full-time education compared to 55 per cent of 17-year-olds in England during 1992–93.

9   Scottish Office Education Department, *The Initial Training of Further Education College Lectures*, Edinburgh, SOED, Review Committee Report, August 1993.

10 S. Targett, 'Employers may back training levy', *Times Higher Education Supplement*, 11 November 1994.

Index